THE Keys TO OVERCOMING

*Unlocking the
Overcomer in You*

CINDY ROOPCHAND

THE Keys TO OVERCOMING

*Unlocking the
Overcomer in You*

CINDY ROOPCHAND

MEWE

Love is the more excellent way

LITHONIA, GA

Publisher:
MEWE, LLC
www.mewellc.com

First Edition
ISBN: 978-1-7324327-7-2

Library of Congress Control Number: 9781732432772

Printed in the United States of America.

This book is dedicated to my husband, my miracle boys, and to all the overcomers. With God all things are possible.

CONTENTS

ALL BELIEVERS HAVE THIS PROMISE EVERYONE BORN OF GOD OVERCOMES THE WORLD. THIS IS THE VICTORY That has overcome the world, EVEN OUR FAITH

1 John 5:4

ACKNOWLEDGEMENTS

I would like to give glory and honor to my Lord and Savior Jesus Christ. Thank you for rescuing me when I was drowning in my sins. Thank you for the blood that you shed for me on Calvary. Thank you for healing and delivering me. Thank you for giving me divine insight, wisdom and revelation. Thank you for your scribe anointing and allowing me to write this book.

I would like to thank my husband for all his support and unconditional love. Thank you for being my best friend and allowing me to be all that God created me to be.

I would like to thank my miracle boys Matthew and Noah. Thank you for being understanding and helping mommy.

I would like to thank my sisters, and my family. Thank you for all your support.

I would like to thank all my prayer warriors and intercessors. Thank you for interceding and warring for me. Thank you for going to the throne room of heaven and petitioning for me. Your prayers, love, and support mean the world to me.

I would like to thank my pastor, my teachers and my church. Thank you for teaching and training me.

I would like to thank my publisher, Minister C. Dudley and the MEWE family for their creativity and helping me bring this book to life.

FOREWORD

Always be aware of who God allows you to cross paths with whether for a five-minute conversation or a lifetime of memories ahead. There's always a reason, a message, a connection that takes place and for me the one created with Cindy Roopchand is continuously flourishing and developing. Cindy and I met about 14 years ago. Our husbands are cousins (more like brothers) and essentially, we gravitated to one another as we were both Bronx girls trying to figure out life. With time the friendship turned into a solid sisterhood full of love, family vacations, business ventures and we realized we had so much in common that at times our lives mirrored one another.

We were blessed to write a book together, be featured in magazines, television shows, and speaking events but nothing is more powerful than our spiritual connection! Although we were both in the world when we met our desires to be free of bondage and walk in our calling brought us both to Christ. We surrendered our lives and began to live for Him. Cindy and I pray together and for one another. We have helped deliver other women spiritually through faith and discipline in hearing Gods voice. To say this book is powerful is truly an understatment.

Having the privilege to see Cindy Roopchand walk in her purpose and propel higher into her calling is a beautiful sight to see. This woman is a firehouse!!! She is poised and reserved but when she opens her mouth no one in the room will leave the same! This book is life changing. It speaks to the depths and core of what true discipleship means. To be connected to a woman who devotes her life to her family and most importantly to sharing the greatness of Jesus Christ is an honor. Be in expectancy, you will Overcome.

This book will open new levels of worship and a dimension of God's word that can only be reached through sound doctrine. You have come across a gem. Both in the book and the author. Enjoy!

Charlyn Nater
Purpose Coach/Motivational Speaker
She Propels, LLC

INTRODUCTION

We are all going to go through some difficult things in life. Difficulties come in all shapes and sizes – sickness, disease, divorce, addictions, fears, and worries can all consume us. Life is unpredictable and it can be a game changer. However, do not lose hope. For the Bible says, "Consider it pure joy, my brothers and sisters whenever you face trials of many kinds, because you know that testing of your faith produces perseverance. Let perseverance finish its work so that you may be mature, and complete, not lacking anything" (James 1:2-4). These trials or troubles came into our lives, not to discourage us but to encourage us to draw nearer to the Lord.

Today, I want you to know that God has called you to be an overcomer! The things you thought were going to take you out are actually going to take you through to the next level. You were not created to be a victim but a victor. Many people want to be victorious and overcome their problems; however, they are not taught how.

This book will teach you how to overcome and be victorious in all areas of your life. My prayer is, after you read this book, that you will not be the same person...that you will choose to walk in the overcoming power that Jesus provided for us on the cross when He shed His blood...that you will be changed, set free, and delivered. I pray that you will discover the inner warrior in you and know that you are more than a conqueror. I know that you will arise knowing that these trials will eventually turn into triumphs.

CHALLENGES

COME

Into Our Lives

TO PUSH US

Out of Our

COMFORT ZONE

And into Our

DESTINIES

Cindy Roopchand

WHO ARE OVERCOMERS?

We are all called to be overcomers. An overcomer is "a person who overcomes something or one who succeeds in dealing with or gaining control of some problem or difficulty." Overcomers are fighters; the word "quit" is not in their vocabulary. You cannot call yourself an overcomer and not have anything to overcome. To overcome is defined as "to succeed in dealing with a problem or difficulty; to defeat (an opponent); to prevail, overpower or overwhelm." To overcome is "to prevail in spite of adversity, to successfully solve a problem or defeat an opponent."

The word "overcome" occurs several times in the New Testament. The Greek word is NIKAO, which means, "to overpower," "to overcome" or "to be victorious." The King's High Way Ministry defines overcomers as "those victorious ones who have learned how to master the flesh, prevail over the world, and conquer the devil only through Christ's Life in them."

KEYS TO BECOMING AN OVERCOMER

Becoming an overcomer is the key to having a successful life. The Bible says, "My people are destroyed for lack of knowledge" (Hosea 4:6). I pray this book will give you the knowledge, the wisdom, the revelation, and the insight you need to be the overcomer God has called you to be.

Keys represent the authority to lock and unlock. I pray the keys I provide for you will unlock the potential in you. My prayer is for you to use these keys and apply them in your life. I pray these keys will open many doors of opportunity. I pray that doors of victory, greatness, blessing, and triumph will open in your life. I pray these keys will release the overcoming and prevailing power in you and through you. That you will become the overcomer God created you to be. Get ready to activate the overcomer in you, unlocking your seeds of greatness. So, let the journey begin...

Get

READY

to

ACTIVATE

the

OVERCOMER

in

YOU...

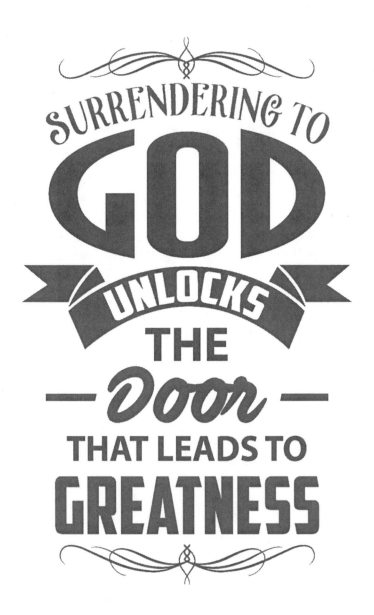

SURRENDERING TO GOD UNLOCKS THE *Door* THAT LEADS TO GREATNESS

1

TOTAL DEPENDENCE ON GOD

The first key to becoming an overcomer is surrendering your life to God. Surrendering means letting go and letting God take over your life. It is when you tell God, "Have Your way!" Surrendering your life is when you totally depend on God. Believe me, I tried to make it on my own and what I found is I could not.

Jesus is the missing piece that completes us. He takes our brokenness and makes us whole. You cannot be who God called you to be without God. If you do not have God in your life, it is like you filming a movie without a director or a script. You need the script, and you need God to direct your life. God created you for a purpose on this earth and He is the only one that can reveal that to you. He will give the skills and the strategies you will need to fulfill your calling.

The Bible says in Jeremiah 1:5, "Before I formed you in the womb, I knew you, before you were born, I set you apart; I appointed you as a prophet to the nations." God knows who you are and has set you apart for great things.

My question to you is, do you know God? If you do not, I invite you to get to know Him. He is your Heavenly Father and He loves you. He longs to reconnect and have a relationship with you. That is why He is called Immanuel, which means "God with us." The Bible says, "Draw near to God, and He will draw near to you" (James 4:8 NKJV). When you accept Jesus Christ as your Lord and Savior, He will become the solution to all your problems. God can do anything but fail you. With God you will lack nothing. He will supply all your needs.

There is One True Living God. He is the God of the Bible and He has many names. Although He is One God, there are so many attributes or dimensions to Him that, in order for us to understand them all, He has given Himself hundreds of names. I believe this is to demonstrate how great our God is. As you read through the following list, I pray you get to know God better and I challenge you to discover some new names of God in the Bible. In addition, I pray that you will make Jesus, your Lord and your Savior. I promise you it will be the best decision you've ever made.

Names of God

- *The Great I AM (Exodus 3:14)*

- *The Alpha and The Omega (Revelation 22:13)*

- *The Beginning and The End (Revelation 22:13)*

- *The First and The Last (Isaiah 48:12)*

- *Healer (Psalm 103.3)*

- *Deliverer (Psalm 70:5)*

- *Redeemer (Isaiah 59:20)*

- *My Strength (Psalm 43:2)*

- *Restorer (Psalm 23:3)*

- *Everlasting Father (Isaiah 9:6)*

- *Love (1 John 4:16)*

- *Strong Tower (Proverbs 18:10)*

- *Living Water (John 4:10)*

- *Bread of Life (John 6:35)*

- *Wonderful Counselor (Isaiah 9:6)*

- *God of Comfort (Romans 15:5)*

- *Lord Who Provides (Genesis 22:14)*

- *Refuge from The Storm (Isaiah 25:14)*

- *Helper (Hebrews 13:6)*

- *Lord of Peace (2 Thessalonians 3:16)*

- *Resting Place (Jeremiah 50:6)*

- *The Giver of Life (Psalm 36:9)*

- *Spirit of Truth (John 16:13)*

- *Husband (Hebrews 13:6)*

- *Hope (Psalm 71:5)*

- *My Shield (Psalm 144:2)*

- *Everlasting Light (Isaiah 60:20)*

KEY PROMISE SCRIPTURE

"Draw near to God, and He will draw near to you"
(James 4:8 NKJV)

Prayer to Unlock

Lord, help me to surrender my life to You and make You my Lord and my Savior. Jesus, help me to totally depend on You and You alone. Remove anything that is not of You. Father God, I ask that You draw near to me, as I draw near to You. I pray that You will give me a Divine revelation of who You really are. I pray that You will open my spiritual eyes to know that You are the One True Living God. That you are the Great I Am, My Provider, My Deliverer, My Comforter, My Healer, and My Father. I need You to be my _____ (Select a name from the list of who you need God to be) today. I thank You, Lord, as I spend time with You, You are transforming me into Your image and likeness. I thank You for the overcoming and victorious power You will pour into my life. I thank You, God, for all that You have and will do for me. I ask these things in the Mighty Name of Jesus Christ. Amen.

Declarations

I Decree and Declare that I will surrender my life to Jesus Christ.

I Decree and Declare that I am depending on Jesus for my breakthrough.

I Decree and Declare that I will draw nearer to God.

I Decree and Declare that God will draw nearer to me.

I Decree and Declare that I will seek the face of God and sit at His feet.

I Decree and Declare that, once I have an encounter with God, I will never be the same in Jesus' name.

I Decree and Declare I am an overcomer through Jesus Christ.

 # Key Points

"Write the vision and make it plain on tablets, that he may run who reads it."
(Habakkuk 2:2 NKJV)

Jot down any key points or key ideas you gained from this section...

Think About It: How can I apply these keys in my life?

_____

_____

_____

_____

_____

_____

_____

_____

_____

_____

_____

_____

_____

_____

_____

_____

_____

_____

Salvation
IS THE GREATEST
Gift one can
Receive

2

SALVATION – COMING INTO COVENANT WITH GOD

The second key to becoming an overcomer is salvation. The Webster Dictionary defines salvation as "the spiritual rescue from the consequences of sin." Salvation is simply God's plan for saving us. It is the steps we need to take for our entrance into the Kingdom of God. Life will teach you that you need to be saved. There will be situations that come into your life where you realize that nobody can help you but God. This is when you run out of options and realize you need to be rescued.

This is what happened to me when I experienced my miscarriage. I was depressed and filled with hopelessness and realized at that moment nobody could help me but God. It was during that dark moment in my life that Jesus, the Light of The World, stepped into my life. Sin, disobedience, rebellion, and problems can all cause us to drown in this life. But I am so thankful that Jesus, my Savior, my Lifeguard, can walk on water.

Someone might ask, "Why do we need to be saved?" First, we need to be saved from sin. The Bible says that there is none righteous; for all have sinned and fallen short of the glory of God" (See Romans 3:10, 23). Secondly, sin separates us from God. We serve a holy God and God cannot fellowship in sin. In addition, the Old Testament states, because Adam sinned, his actions disconnected us from God. Sin affects our relationship with God. Sin can open the door to the enemy and block our blessings.

Finally, we need salvation because we need to be saved from death. Romans 6:23 says "For the wages of sin is death; but the gift of God is eternal life through Jesus Christ our

Lord." Sin brings everlasting consequences but, thank God, Jesus brings everlasting life.

Salvation is God's plan for separating us from our sins and reuniting us with Himself. It is how we come into covenant with God. A covenant is an agreement, a pact, or a contract. There are countless benefits available to all who come into covenant with God.

The following two scriptures describe God's Salvation plan for us. John 3:16 (KJV) states: "For God so loved the world that he gave his only begotten Son, that whosoever **believeth** in him should not perish, but have everlasting life." Acts 2:38 (KJV) says, "Then Peter said unto them, **Repent**, and be **baptized** every one of you in the name of Jesus Christ for the remission of sins, and ye shall receive the **Gift of the Holy Ghost**." According to the above scriptures, there are four steps in God's salvation plan for us. They include **Faith in God, Repentance, Water Baptism,** and **Receiving the Holy Spirit**.

God's Salvation plan for us is considered our "New Birth" experience or how we become "Born again" believers. Think about the birthing experience in a physical birth; there are certain steps that need to be taken in order for the baby to survive. For instance, the mother has to deliver the baby from her body. Next, the baby has to breathe or draw breath from its lungs. After that, the umbilical cord needs to be cut. If any of these steps is omitted, the baby won't survive.

The same is true of our spiritual birth. All of these steps have to take place to complete our spiritual birth. I will briefly discuss these steps but will go into more depth about each of them in the following chapters.

The first step in the plan of salvation is **Faith.** You need to believe in Jesus and accept Him as your Savior (Redeemer) and Lord (Ruler). The Bible says, "If you declare with your mouth, 'Jesus is Lord,' and believe in your heart that God raised him from the dead, you will be saved. For it is with your heart that you believe and are justified, and it is with your mouth that you profess your faith and are saved" (Romans 10:9-10). "

Believe on the Lord Jesus Christ, and thou shalt be saved, and thy house" (Acts 16:31 KJV). "Neither is there salvation in any other, for there is none other name under heaven given among men, whereby we must be saved" (Acts 4:12 KJV).

The second step is **Repentance.** This is when you ask for forgiveness of your sins and you are turning away from them. Jesus says in Luke 13:5 (KJV), "I tell you, Nay; but, except ye repent, ye shall all likewise perish."

The third step is **Water Baptism.** This is when you are immersed in water in Jesus' name for the forgiveness of your sins. Acts 22:16 (KJV) says, "Arise and be baptized, and wash away thy sins, calling on the name of the Lord."

The fourth step is being filled with the **Holy Spirit,** which means having God's Spirit living within us. Romans 8:11 (KJV) states, "But if the Spirit of him that raised up Jesus from the dead dwell in you, he that raised up Christ from the dead shall also quicken your mortal bodies by his Spirit that dwelleth in you."

Salvation is a free gift from God, and it is available for you today. Ephesians 2:7-9 says that the reason for this is: "...that in the coming ages he might show the incomparable riches of his grace, expressed in his kindness to us in Christ Jesus. For it is by grace you have been saved, through faith— and this is not from yourselves, it is the gift of God not by works, so that no one can boast."

It is crucial to remember we cannot earn our salvation by good works. We cannot buy or earn our way into heaven. When we try to earn our way to heaven, we become prideful, judgmental and independent. When we deny God's complete work, we start to think of ourselves as being perfect, like God, and this is a form of idolatry God will not accept.

The Bible says, "We are all infected and impure with sin. When we display our righteous deeds, they are nothing but filthy rags. Like autumn leaves, we wither and fall, and our sins sweep us away like the wind" (Isaiah 64:6 NLT). Another translation says our good works are like "polluted garments." The Bible is making it clear that our "perfect" work is not good enough for a Perfect God.

I am so grateful God did all the work of salvation and He made it available for all. God is offering this free gift to you. The choice to receive God's salvation is the single most important decision you will make in your lifetime. I pray that you will accept it today.

KEY PROMISE SCRIPTURE

"Then Peter said unto them, Repent, and be baptized every one of you in the name of Jesus Christ for the remission of sins, and ye shall receive the Gift of the Holy Ghost"
(Acts 2:38 KJV)

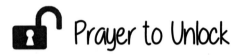 Prayer to Unlock

Father God, thank You so much for the gift of salvation. Help me to be obedient and come into covenant with You. Help me to surrender to You, to Your Word, and to Your Will for My life. Your word shows me the steps I need to take in order to be saved. Help me to walk by faith and believe in Your wonder-working power. Give me the desire to repent and turn away from sin, in Jesus' Name. Remove the spiritual scales from my eyes and let me see the Truth. Jesus, I accept You as my Lord and my Savior. I will be baptized in Jesus' Name and I will be filled with the Holy Spirit. Thank You for Your Redemptive Plan and for giving me access to it through the Blood of Jesus. By faith, I graciously receive the gift of salvation. I claim it now, in Jesus' Precious Name. Amen.

Declarations

I Decree and Declare that I will be saved in Jesus' Name.

I Decree and Declare that I will come into covenant with God.

I Decree and Declare that I will be obedient to the Lord and I will follow His Salvation Plan.

I Decree and Declare that Jesus is Lord and Savior over my life.

 Key Points

"Write the vision and make it plain on tablets, that he may run who reads it."
(Habakkuk 2:2 NKJV)

Jot down any key points or key ideas you gained from this section...

Think About It: How can I apply these keys in my life?

_____

_____

_____

_____

_____

_____

_____

_____

_____

FAITH IS HAVING A HEAVENLY PERSPECTIVE

CINDY ROOPCHAND

3

FAITH – HEAVEN'S CURRENCY

The third key to becoming an overcomer is to have faith in God. The Bible says, "Without faith it is impossible to please God, because anyone who comes to him must believe that he exists and that he rewards those who earnestly seek him" (Hebrews 11:6).

Faith is defined as "complete trust or confidence in someone or something." To have faith is simply to believe. In order to receive you must believe.

The Bible states, "now faith is the substance of things hoped for, the evidence of things not seen" (Hebrews 11:1 KJV). You have to believe in God and in what He says regardless of your circumstances. You have to depend and rely solely upon Him. I always say you need to put on your "faith goggles" and see things the way God does.

Faith means putting your total trust and confidence in God and in His Word. The Bible states that our faith must remain constant and steadfast (See 1 Corinthians 16:13). This means we begin with faith and end with faith.

The Scripture declares that God has dealt to each one a measure of faith (See Romans 12:3). In other words, God has given each of us some faith to start with. However, we need to seek and ask God to build our faith. This is why it is crucial for us to increase our faith daily.

The Bible states, "Faith comes by hearing and hearing by the word of God" (Romans 10:17 NKJV). God can only work through your faith. Faith is heaven's currency, so, if you want things to shift in your life, you must have faith. Scripture says, "If you have faith as small as a mustard seed, you can say to this mountain, 'Move from here to there,' and it will move. Nothing will be impossible for you." (Matthew 17:20 NIV). Mountains can represent problems, difficulties, troubles, and trials. In order to remove these obstacles in our way, we need to have faith. It is important to ask the Lord to increase your faith and to teach you how to walk by faith, not by sight (See 2 Corinthians 5:7) so you can move mountains, too.

KEY PROMISE SCRIPTURE

"Without faith it is impossible to please God, because anyone who comes to him must believe that he exists and that he rewards those who earnestly seek him"
(Hebrews 11:6)

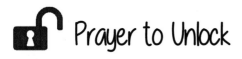 Prayer to Unlock

Father God, in the Name of Jesus, I ask that You anoint me with a Faith mantle. That You will pour down Your supernatural faith upon me. That I will no longer walk by my feelings, but by my faith. I will walk by faith and not by sight. That every time I read the Word of God; my faith will increase. I ask that every time I speak the Word of God, my faith will grow. I declare that every time I hear Your Word, my faith will multiply. I thank You, God, that every time I exercise my Faith muscle, I will be stronger

in my walk with You. I thank You, God, that You will grant me the faith to move mountains and do the impossible. I thank You, God, that You are tripling my faith portion as I stay true to You and to Your Word. I ask these things in Jesus' Mighty Name, Amen.

Declarations

I Decree and Declare that I will walk by faith and not by sight.

I Decree, and I Declare that my faith is increasing daily.

I Decree and Declare that I will read the Word of God and build my Faith.

I Decree and Declare that I will hear the Word of God and it will deepen my faith.

I Decree and Declare I have a Faith mantle upon my life.

I Decree and Declare my faith in God will allow me to do the impossible in Jesus' Name.

 **Key Points**

"Write the vision and make it plain on tablets, that he may run who reads it."
(Habakkuk 2:2 NKJV)

Jot down any key points or key ideas you gained from this section...

Think About It: How can I apply these keys in my life?

_____
_____
_____
_____
_____
_____
_____
_____
_____
_____
_____
_____
_____
_____
_____
_____
_____
_____

FORGIVENESS

is a key that

FREES YOU TO WALK

INTO YOUR

FREEDOM

— CINDY ROOPCHAND —

4

FORGIVENESS LEADS TO YOUR FREEDOM

The fourth key to becoming an overcomer is forgiveness. There is power in forgiveness. In order to be an overcomer, you need to be forgiven and you need to forgive others.

We all make mistakes. No one is perfect but God. The Bible says that "all have sinned and fall short of the glory of God" (Romans 3:23). Sin puts us in bondage. It opens the door for the enemy to work in our lives. Sin can lead us down the path of destruction. "For the wages of sin is death" (Romans 6:23). Sin separates us from God, and it can block our prayers from being answered. The Bible says, "Your iniquities have separated you from God; and your sins have hidden his face from you, so that he will not hear" (Isaiah 59:2). The Bible mentions there is an eternal consequence for sin: "The one who sins is the one who will die" (Ezekiel 18:20). This is why we need to be saved from our sins, and I thank God that Jesus is our Savior.

We all need to confess and repent of our sins because of Adam's disobedience. All humans are born in sin (See Psalm 51:5) and no matter how "good" we try to be, we have all sinned. We have to remember sin includes our thoughts and actions. Doubt, anger, unbelief, and selfishness are all forms of sin.

The first step is to name each sin you can remember, admit you are wrong, and ask for God's forgiveness. "If we confess our sins, he is faithful and just to forgive us our sins, and to cleanse us from all unrighteousness" (1 John 1:9 KJV). It is critical that we not only confess our sins, but we also experience repentance. Confessing is acknowledging our sins, while repenting is turning away from them.

26

Think of children. They may sometimes cry after they have done something wrong, but they may only cry because they got caught. Repentance begins with being sorry; however, it also involves you changing your thinking and behavior. Repentance is symbolic of "dying to sin" and "crucifying the old you." It's when you put to death your old self and become a new creature in Christ that your transformation begins.

The Bible says we will have to give an account of our lives. The sooner we get things right with God, the better it will be for us. Sin is so heavy; it can weigh us down. That's why it is important to confess every sin as soon as we are aware of it. I believe it is important to confess your sins daily and to ask the Lord to reveal any sin you might not be aware of. I encourage you to read Psalm 51. Here are a few verses from it:

"Have mercy upon me, O God, according to your loving kindness; according to the multitude of your tender mercies, blot out my transgression. Wash me thoroughly from my iniquity and cleanse me from my sin." (Psalm 51:1-2 KJV).

"Create in me a clean heart and renew a right spirit within me. Do not cast me away from your presence, and do not take your Holy Spirit away from me" (Psalm 51:10-11 KJV).

Just as God has forgiven you, you need to forgive others. Jesus says, "Judge not, and you shall not be judged. Condemn not, and you shall not be condemned. Forgive, and you will be forgiven" (Luke 6:37 NKJV). Mark 11:25 says, "Whenever you stand praying, if you have anything against anyone, forgive him so that your Father in heaven may also forgive you your sins." He also says, in Matthew 6:14-15, "For if you forgive other people when they sin against you, your heavenly Father will also forgive you. But if you do not forgive others their sins, your Father will not forgive your sins."

Jesus teaches us that if we want God to forgive us, we need to forgive others. When we choose not to forgive, we end up walking in the dark (See 1 John 2:9-11) and blocking our blessings. I know I cannot be a light to others as long as I am walking in the darkness of unforgiveness. Remember, your forgiving someone does not justify their actions or make them right; but it does make you free. Forgiveness releases the one who wronged you into God's hands so that He can deal with them. Forgiveness is the best revenge because it not only sets us free from the person, but it frees us into all that God has for us.

We all have been hurt at some point. I remember growing up and experiencing a lot of disappointment. I grew up in a broken home and witnessed a lot of pain at a young age. Therefore, it is important to look back in order to move forward.

So, first of all, make sure you have forgiven your parents or close family members. The Bible says, "Honor your father and your mother, so that you may live long in the land the Lord your God is giving you" (Exodus 20:12). You cannot honor your parents if you bear unforgiveness towards them and, believe me, you do not want to shorten your life. Forgive them and ask God to restore your relationship with them. I know He did it for me and He will surely do it for you.

Jesus told us to love God and to love others. The best way you can love others is by forgiving them. Peter asked Jesus, "Lord, how many times shall I forgive my brother or sister who sins against me? Up to seven times?" Jesus answered, "I tell you, not seven times, but seventy-seven times" (Matthew 18:21, 22). That is 490 times a day! God is making the point to forgive someone as many times as is necessary. He is emphasizing the importance of forgiveness. Remember, forgiveness is a choice we need to make every day.

I know forgiving someone might not be easy. But, remember, forgiveness doesn't excuse their behavior. It prevents their behavior from destroying your heart. When you choose to forgive those who have hurt you, you take away their power. Some things that I have done to help me become a forgiving person were, first, I asked God to help me have a forgiving heart. Next, I asked God to soften my heart towards my offenders and I asked God to soften their hearts towards me. Lastly, I prayed for them because the Bible says we must love our enemies.

A huge part of moving into all that God has for us involves forgiving others. Do not let unforgiveness limit what God wants to do in your life. So today, I encourage you to let go and let God handle it.

KEY PROMISE SCRIPTURE

*"If you forgive men their trespasses, your heavenly
Father will also forgive you. But if you do not forgive
men their trespasses, neither will your Father forgive
your trespasses"*
(Matthew 6:14-15 ESV)

🔓 Prayer to Unlock

*Your Word says in 1 John 1:9, "If we confess our sins,
He is faithful and just and will forgive us our sins and
purify us from all unrighteousness." Father God, I am a
sinner. I confess my sins to You. (Repent and confess out
loud every sin you committed and ask God to forgive
you). I realize my prayers cannot save me; only You can.
So, I thank You for the Blood that You shed on Calvary.
Your Blood has redeemed me and washed away all my
sins. The Blood of Jesus brings forgiveness. I thank You
for Your forgiveness power. Your Word says, "For if you
forgive other people when they sin against you, your
heavenly Father will also forgive you. But if you do not
forgive others their sins, your Father will not forgive
your sins" (Matthew 6:14-15). Help me forgive and set
(name anyone who has offended you) free. I release them
to You. Heal me of the pain and help me to bless those
who have hurt me. I choose to forgive others just as You
have forgiven me. In Jesus' name, Amen.*

Declarations

I Decree and Declare that I am forgiven.

I Decree and Declare that I will forgive others.

I Decree and Declare that I will confess my sins daily.

I Decree and Declare I will walk in the forgiveness Jesus died to give me.

I Decree and Declare I will let go of all unforgiveness and bitterness.

I Decree and Declare that God will give me a forgiving heart filled with His love.

 Key Points

"Write the vision and make it plain on tablets, that he may run who reads it. "
(Habakkuk 2:2 NKJV)

Jot down any key points or key ideas you gained from this section...

Think About It: How can I apply these keys in my life?

_____

_____

_____

_____

_____

WATER BAPTISM

THE SUPER CLEANSING

POWER OF

JESUS

CHRIST

CINDY ROOPCHAND

5

WATER BAPTISM –
THE CLEANSING POWER

The fifth key to becoming an overcomer is water baptism. You may ask, "Why should I be baptized?" Water Baptism symbolically washes away all of your sins. The Bible says, "Arise and be baptized, and wash away thy sins, calling on the name of the Lord" (Acts 22:16 KJV). Water makes you clean, so don't you want a clean slate with God? If Jesus Christ, the only man without sin, humbled Himself to be baptized in water, then certainly we need to be baptized, too. Baptism is our spiritual washing. It is a step we must follow to tell the world we are with Christ.

The Bible says in John 3:5 (KJV), "Except a man be born of water and of the Spirit, he cannot enter into the kingdom of God." The Book of Acts 2:38 says, "Repent and be baptized, every one of you" and Acts 19:5 states, "...they were baptized in the name of the Lord Jesus..." Mark 16:15-16 (KJV) says, "And he said unto them, 'Go ye into all of the world, and preach the gospel to every creature. He that believeth and is baptized shall be saved; but he that believeth not shall be damned.'" As you can see from these Scriptures, baptism is a direct command from Jesus.

Water Baptism is a part of our "new birth" experience. When a mother gives birth to a child in the natural, there is always water and blood involved. Well, in your spiritual birth you must have water and blood, too, which is water baptism and the blood of Jesus. We should be baptized because baptism identifies us as being buried with Jesus Christ. Romans 6:3-4 (KJV) says, "Know ye not, that so many of us as were baptized into Jesus Christ were baptized into his death? Therefore, we are buried with him by baptism into death: that as Christ was raised up from the dead by the glory of the Father, even so we also should walk in newness of life."

The Apostle Paul describes baptism as a burial. Just as repentance represents the "death" of your old self, so baptism represents the "burial." When something dies you need to bury it. Baptism is when you are "burying your old self or life" so that a new person can be born into eternal life. For the Bible says, we become new creatures in Christ (See 2 Corinthians 5:17).

Another reason we should be baptized is because it marks us as recipients of the New Covenant in Christ Jesus. Jesus provided a new covenant in His blood (agreement, contract) as mentioned in Luke 22:20. In Colossians 2:11 the Apostle Paul explains this new covenant does not require the outward cutting away of physical flesh like the covenant God made with Abraham. However, this new covenant requires the inward cutting away of sin in the heart.

The Scripture says: "In him [Jesus Christ] you were also circumcised with a circumcision not performed by human hands. Your whole self ruled by the flesh was put off when you were circumcised by Christ, having been buried with him in baptism, in which you were also raised with him through your faith in the working of God, who raised Him from the dead. When you were dead in your sins and in the uncircumcision of your flesh, God made you alive with Christ. He forgave us all our sins ..." (Colossians 2:11-13 NIV).

The Apostle Paul is saying that, just as circumcision was the mark of the old covenant, so is water baptism the mark of the new covenant. Water baptism symbolizes our participation in the new covenant with Jesus Christ.

Baptism is a divine command from Jesus Christ. Baptism brings us into the new covenant with Christ and is a privilege, a blessing, and a responsibility. Water Baptism is an important part of our new birth experience. It is a spiritual washing of our sins. When you come into covenant with Jesus Christ, you are guaranteed many benefits.

KEY PROMISE SCRIPTURE

"Except a man be born of water and of the Spirit, he cannot enter into the kingdom of God"
(John 3:5 KJV)

 Prayer to Unlock

Lord, I humbly thank You for Your precious gift of water baptism. I thank You for the cleansing power it brings in my life. My sins are washed away with the Blood of Jesus. Thank You for Your salvation plan and for the new birth experience. As I step into the water of baptism, I bury my old self and become a new creature in Christ. I thank You that, once I step out of the water, I stand free, forgiven, whole and loved. My past is gone, and my God-

given future awaits me. I am a born again believer. I am a daughter or son of the King of Kings and Lord of Lords. I boldly and confidently walk into my new life with Christ. In Jesus' name, Amen.

Declarations

I Decree and Declare that my sins will be washed away by the Blood of Jesus.

I Decree and Declare that I will be obedient to be baptized in Jesus' name.

I Decree and Declare that God's cleansing power is upon me.

I Decree and Declare I am a new creature in Christ.

 Key Points

"Write the vision and make it plain on tablets, that he may run who reads it."
(Habakkuk 2:2 NKJV)

Jot down any key points or key ideas you gained from this section...

Think About It: How can I apply these keys in my life?

_____

_____

_____

_____

_____

HOLY SPIRIT
YOUR
— INNER —
COMPASS
— FOR —
Life
Cindy Roopchand

6

HOLY SPIRIT – GOD'S SPIRIT DWELLING IN YOU

The sixth key to becoming an overcomer is receiving the Holy Spirit. The Holy Spirit is the Spirit of Christ dwelling or living in you. It is power being released from heaven. Before Jesus' death, burial, and resurrection, He promised that He would not leave His disciples comfortless or alone. He promised to send them the Holy Spirit, who would give them power from "on high" (See Acts 2:33).

"And I will pray the Father, and he shall give you another Comforter, that he may abide with you forever; Even the Spirit of truth; whom the world cannot receive, because it seeth him not, neither knoweth him: but ye know him; for he dwelleth with you, and shall be in you. I will not leave you comfortless: I will come to you" (John 14:16-18 KJV). "But the Comforter, which is the Holy Ghost, whom the Father will send in my name, he shall teach you all things, and bring all things to your remembrance, whatsoever I have said unto you" (John 14:26 KJV). Jesus was promising to return to His disciples in another way or manifestation. He would no longer be with them "in the flesh" or in the natural, but He would return to them "in the Spirit" through the Holy Spirit living in them.

This promise was fulfilled on the day of Pentecost. Acts Chapter 2:1-4 describes this dramatic event: "When the day of Pentecost came, they were all together in one place. Suddenly a sound like the blowing of a violent wind came from heaven and filled the whole house where they were sitting. They saw what seemed to be tongues of fire that separated and came to rest on each of them. All of them were filled with the Holy Spirit and began to speak in other tongues as the Spirit enabled them."

From the above Scripture, you can see God was imparting spiritual life into us. He was giving us His Spirit to be a witness on this earth for Him. On this day, Peter the Apostle received transformation power. Peter had denied knowing Christ before His crucifixion, but, once He became filled with the Spirit, he preached a bold and anointed sermon that led to the conversion of 3,000 souls that day (See Acts 2:41). This was the birth of the early church.

There are many reasons we need the Holy Spirit. First, it is part of God's salvation plan for us. It is how we enter into covenant with the Lord. Titus 3:5 states, "He saved us, not because of righteous things we had done, but because of his mercy. He saved us through the washing of rebirth and renewal by the Holy Spirit." This Scripture mentions the two elements we need to be saved: washing (water baptism) and the renewal by the Holy Spirit (Holy Spirit infilling).

John 3:5 says, "Jesus answered, 'Very truly I tell you, no one can enter the kingdom of God unless they are born of water and the Spirit.'" Therefore, the Holy Spirit is part of our new birth experience. Romans 8:11 tells us that the Holy Spirit gives us resurrection (quickening) power: "And if the Spirit of him who raised Jesus from the dead is living in you, he who raised Christ from the dead will also give life to your mortal bodies because of his Spirit who lives in you."

The Bible says the Holy Spirit provides many benefits for us. "But the Advocate, the Holy Spirit, whom the Father will send in my name, will teach you all things and will remind you of everything I have said to you" (John 14:26). The Holy Spirit is the Spirit of Truth who teaches us the things of God or spiritual things. John 16:13 declares that the Holy Spirit will "guide us in all truth." Romans 8:26-27 states that the Holy Spirit helps us to discern, pray and intercede, all of which cause us to be effective prayer warriors. The Book of Acts 1:8 and 4:31 tells us the Holy Spirit gives us power and boldness. Romans 8:9 says that the Holy Spirit identifies us as belonging to God. 2 Corinthians 3:17 declares that the Holy Spirit frees us and gives us liberty. 1 Corinthians 12:4-13 tells us the Holy Spirit imparts spiritual gifts. Galatians 5:22-25 describes how the Holy Spirit empowers us to bear spiritual fruit or the fruit of the Spirit. Mark 13:11 explains how the Holy Spirit gives us wisdom when we face difficult situations.

Please note the Holy Spirit is for everyone. The Bible says in Joel 2:28 that the Spirit will be poured upon "all flesh." In addition, Acts 2:39 says, "For the promise is unto you, and to your children, and to all that are afar off, even as many as the Lord our God shall call." In Acts 10:34-35 the Apostle Peter states that people of every nation are eligible to receive the Holy Spirit. The Holy Spirit is a gift from God, given to those who ask (See Acts 2:38; Luke 11:13) and to those who obey Him (See Acts 5:32). If you hunger and thirst for the Holy Spirit, God will surely give Him to you.

You need God's Spirit in you to fight the battles ahead of you. His Spirit gives us the power and the strength to be true overcomers. The Holy Spirit brings transformation power. Before I received the Holy Spirit, I was timid, shy and fearful. After I got filled with the Holy Spirit, I became bold and confident. Only through the Spirit of Christ did I become victorious. I know you will, too.

KEY PROMISE SCRIPTURE

"And afterward,
I will pour out my Spirit on all people.
Your sons and daughters will prophesy,
your old men will dream dreams,
your young men will see visions"
(Joel 2:28)

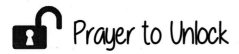 Prayer to Unlock

Heavenly Father, I thank You for saving me. I pray that Your Holy Spirit descend upon me right now. Baptize me now with the Holy Ghost. I am hungry and desperate for Your Spirit. Fill me with Your Spirit in a mighty way. Pour down Your Spirit upon all flesh. May we be Spirit-led all the days of our life. I receive the baptism in the Holy Spirit right now by faith. May the anointing, the glory, and the power of God come upon me right now. I thank You for the Holy Spirit living and dwelling in me. Thank You for the boldness and confidence the Spirit of God brings into my life. May the Holy Ghost fire fall upon me in a powerful way. Holy Spirit, rain down on me. I thank You for baptizing me with the Holy Spirit. From this day I am empowered to do all that You have called me to do. I ask these things in Jesus' name, Amen.

Declarations

I Decree and Declare that I will be filled with God's Spirit and power.

I Decree and Declare that I will receive the Holy Spirit with the evidence of speaking in other tongues.

I Decree and Declare I will walk in the boldness and confidence of the Holy Ghost.

I Decree and Declare I have the Holy Ghost fire in Me.

I Decree and Declare the Holy Ghost will teach me everything I need to know.

I Decree and Declare the Holy Ghost will lead me and guide me as long as I shall live.

 Key Points

"Write the vision and make it plain on tablets, that he may run who reads it."
(Habakkuk 2:2 NKJV)

Jot down any key points or key ideas you gained from this section...

Think About It: How can I apply these keys in my life?

_____

_____

_____

_____

_____

_____

THE WORD OF GOD is WISDOM TO LIVE BY

Cindy Roopchand

7

THE WORD OF GOD – KNOWLEDGE IS POWER

The seventh key to becoming an overcomer is the Word of God. "Man shall not live by bread alone, but by every word that comes from the mouth of God" (Luke 4:4). If you want to survive and thrive, you need to feed yourself physically and spiritually. The Bible is our spiritual "daily bread." The Word of God, the Bible, gives us the necessary vitamins and nutrients we need to grow spiritually. It builds our faith and gives us the strength to be overcomers. "So, then faith comes by hearing and hearing by the word of God" (Romans 10:17 NKJV). If you want to know the mind of God, the will of God, and the heart of God, then you have to get into the Word of God.

It is important to know that the Bible is not a history book, but it is the Living Word of God present in the here-and-now. It is God speaking to us. It is pure and absolute truth. John 1:1, 14 (KJV) states, "In the beginning was the Word, and the Word was with God, and the Word was God ... And the Word was made flesh and dwelt among us." This Scripture confirms that the Word of God is Jesus Christ in written manifestation.

"All Scripture is given by inspiration of God and is profitable for doctrine, for reproof, for correction, for instruction in righteousness" (2 Timothy 3:16 KJV). This scripture confirms that every word was written under God's divine inspiration and anointing. It also states the numerous benefits from reading the Word. The Bible teaches us about God and how to be overcomers. It corrects us and ensures us that we are walking in the path God has for us. "Thy word is a

50

lamp unto my feet, and a light unto my path" (Psalm 119:105 KJV).

The Bible is relevant today because it is timeless, unchanging, and everlasting. "The grass withers, and the flowers fade, but the word of God stands forever" (Isaiah 40:8 NLT). Jesus said in Matthew 24:35, "Heaven and earth will pass away but my words will never pass away."

The Bible not only gives us knowledge but equips us to be all that God created us to be. Psalm 33:6 (KJV) demonstrates the creative power God released through the Word when it says, "By the word of the Lord were the heavens made." Psalm 107:20 (KJV) declares God's healing power being released through the Word: "He sent His word, and healed them, and delivered them from their destructions."

The Word of God gives us the revelation and the insight to know the ways of God and to be wise in making decisions. The Word of God is our handbook for spiritual training. The Bible imparts God's instructions on how we should live. It provides us with direction when we are lost. The Bible also gives us the answers to the problems in our lives.

The Word of God brings an abundance of spiritual riches. The Bible makes us wise or gives us spiritual knowledge. Proverbs 2:6 states, "For the Lord gives wisdom; out of his mouth comes knowledge and understanding." The Book of Proverbs gives us invaluable advice to help us over difficulties. The Bible gives us the peace that passes all understanding, especially when we are walking through the storms of life.

Most importantly, the Word of God gives us overcoming power. It is our spiritual weapon. Ephesians 6:17 calls it "the sword of the Spirit, which is the word of God." When the enemy tried to tempt Jesus in the wilderness, Jesus used the Word of God as His weapon to defeat him. Three times Jesus defeated the enemy's attack by saying "It is written..." He overcame and won the victory by quoting the Word of God. If our Savior, Jesus used the Word to overcome, then we must, too.

KEY PROMISE SCRIPTURE

"All scripture is given by inspiration of God, and is profitable for doctrine, for reproof, for correction, for instruction in righteousness"
(2 Timothy 3:16 KJV)

Prayer to Unlock

Thank You, Heavenly Father for Your Word. We know every word was written under Your divine inspiration and anointing. Thank You for the numerous benefits it gives us. Thank You for teaching us how to be victorious overcomers through your Word. God, help me to prioritize Your Word in my life. Give me revelation and insight as I read it every day. Speak to me through Your Word, God. Teach me, God, how to use it as my weapon to defeat the enemy. May Your Word draw me nearer to You. In Jesus' Name, Amen.

Declarations

I Decree and Declare that I will stay in the Word of God so that I may have the Mind of God.

I Decree and Declare I will read the Word of God every day.

I Decree and Declare I will use the Bible as my guide all the days of my life.

I Decree and Declare I will speak the Word of God.

I Decree and Declare the Word of God will give me overcoming power to win every battle.

 Key Points

"Write the vision and make it plain on tablets, that he may run who reads it. "
(Habakkuk 2:2 NKJV)

Jot down any key points or key ideas you gained from this section...

Think About It: How can I apply these keys in my life?

_____
_____
_____
_____
_____
_____
_____

THE BLOOD OF JESUS

RELEASES OVERCOMING

POWER

CINDY ROOPCHAND

8

THE BLOOD OF JESUS –
YOUR SPIRITUAL DNA

The eighth key to becoming an overcomer is the Blood of Jesus. There is wonder-working power in the Blood of Jesus. In order to be an overcomer, you need to use and apply the blood of Jesus over your life. If people would open their spiritual eyes and have a revelation of what the blood of Jesus does for us, they would be blown away. The blood of Jesus provides us with amazing spiritual benefits. It has redeemed or bought back things that were stolen from us. The blood of Jesus is so powerful that it breaks all curses, sicknesses and diseases. No power on earth can match the blood of Jesus.

Revelation 12:11 declares, "They overcame by the blood of the Lamb and the word of their testimony." This Scripture clearly shows that, if you want to be an overcomer, you need the blood of the Lamb. In the Old Testament when Adam sinned by disobeying God and obeying the enemy, this caused a separation between man and God. However, God in His mercy, already had a plan to reunite us with Him. This plan involved the shedding of blood as payment for our sins.

Blood represents death and life. Something had to die in order for something to live. In the past, God had allowed the death of a spotless animal to take the place of a sinner. Hebrews 9:22 states, "In fact, the law requires that nearly everything be cleansed with blood, and without the shedding of blood there is no forgiveness." Since we all fall short of God's standard and sin daily, this Old Testament covenant was only temporary because the blood of animals needed to be shed daily and even annually. But, thank God for Jesus, who provided us with a new and better covenant!

The Bible calls Jesus "the Lamb of God, who takes away the sins of the world" (John 1:29 NKJV). Jesus died on the cross and shed His blood for those who put their faith in Him. This act of His dying in the place of all sinners was a sacrifice that would never have to be repeated. Hebrews 7:27 states, "Unlike the other high priests, he does not need to offer sacrifices day after day, first for his own sins, and then for the sins of the people. He sacrificed for their sins once and for all when he offered himself." His blood purchased our forgiveness and freedom from death once-and-for-all.

The blood of Jesus Christ is the most precious gift God can offer us. The Apostle Peter wrote, "For you know that God paid a ransom to save you from the empty life you inherited from your ancestors. And the ransom he paid was not mere gold or silver. He paid for you with the precious lifeblood of Christ, the sinless, spotless Lamb of God" (1 Peter 1:18-19 NLT).

At the cross Jesus regained for us healing, peace, and forgiveness of our sins. Isaiah 53:5 (KJV) states: "But he was wounded for our transgressions, he was bruised for our iniquities: the chastisement of our peace was upon him; and with his stripes we are healed."

Apostle Paul A. Williams wrote an amazing article that discusses the seven places where Jesus shed His blood and their significance. This gave me powerful insight into what the blood of Jesus has purchased for us. I would like to briefly discuss these seven places and what they mean for us. You can find the link to this article in my notes section.

The first place in which Jesus shed His blood was the Garden of Gethsemane when He was praying. "And being in anguish, he prayed more earnestly, and his sweat was like drops of blood falling to the ground" (Luke 22:44). He prayed, asking for the cup of suffering He was going to meet at the cross, to be removed from Him. Nevertheless, He said, not His will but the Father's will be done. Remember, it was in the Garden of Eden that Adam sinned and surrendered his will-power to satan. It was in this Garden of Gethsemane that Jesus redeemed our will-power to say no to sin.

The second place Jesus shed His blood was at the whipping post. He redeemed our health while being whipped. Do you know that the 39 lashes He received represent 39 root-diseases in the world? Each one of those beatings was for a particular sickness-group a person could ever suffer from.

When we participate in Holy Communion, we are remembering the sacrifice Jesus made for us on the cross. The breaking of bread is a reminder of how Jesus' body was broken for our healing so that we could be made whole. When we drink of the cup at Communion, it reminds us of the blood Jesus shed for us on Calvary. Now we can have Jesus' healing power and DNA flowing through us and in us.

Remember, there is no sickness that the blood of Jesus cannot heal because Jesus paid for it all. Isaiah 53:5 says, "With His stripes we are healed." Don't ever let the doctor or anyone tell you that you cannot be healed. Jesus healed everyone that came to Him, and today He wants to heal you. So, claim your healing today in Jesus' name.

The next place where Jesus shed His blood was internally from the wounds He received at the whipping post. Jesus brought back forgiveness and liberty for our transgressions and iniquities. Transgression is our willingness to sin; it is willful sin, knowing that we are sinning. Iniquities are generational curses, which are sins we inherited from our natural parents or ancestors. For example, if my dad was a worrier, then most likely I will become a worrier, too. Jesus freed us from our sins, transgressions and iniquities. Jesus shed His blood and died so we don't have to be a slave to sin anymore. I want you to know that the grip of sin cannot be too great for God.

Jesus shed His blood again when they put the crown of thorns on His head. When Jesus began to shed blood from His head, He was restoring our peace of mind and healing us from all mental torment. Jesus was protecting our minds from all the spiritual attacks the enemy attempts to launch at us. Jesus knows the enemy likes to attack our minds because if, He has our mind, He has our life. Mental sickness or disease, like depression, stress, anxiety, schizophrenia and double-mindedness, has serious effects on people. Jesus set our minds free. He liberated us and broke all mental strongholds and bondages when the crown of thorns pierced His head.

Jesus shed His blood again when they pierced His hands. With the blood oozing from the palms of Jesus, He was redeeming our power to be successful, prosperous, and have the ability to claim our spiritual inheritance. Jesus was taking away the curse on our hands so that everything we touch will prosper and succeed. Now our hands are no longer cursed because Jesus hung on a tree and died for us. Our hands have been washed and purified by the blood of Jesus; because His hands were wounded, our hands can be blessed.

Jesus also shed His blood when they pierced His feet. Here, Jesus redeemed our dominion and authority. Everywhere we walk and what we tread on is ours because God gave us His dominion. Dominion is in the place of our feet. This is where we subject every power that rises against us. Anything that is under your feet is under your power. God says, "Every place that the sole of your foot shall tread upon, that have I given unto you ..." (Joshua 1:3 KJV). Luke 10:19 says," I have given you authority to trample on snakes and scorpions and to overcome all the power of the enemy; nothing will harm you." This is dominion.

Through the blood Jesus shed when they nailed His feet on the cross, our feet have also been cleansed of all manner of defilement. Now we are able to stand before the enemy, to resist him, and to demand that he give back what is ours.

Finally, Jesus shed His blood when they pierced His side. When His side was pierced, water and blood flowed out. This is to demonstrate that Jesus died of a broken heart. Can you imagine how He felt hanging on that cross, being denied, betrayed, humiliated, cursed at, and spat upon? Because Jesus' heart was broken, our heart can be made new. He restored our joy and healed every broken heart. The Bible says He has turned our mourning into dancing and given us beauty for ashes (see Psalm 30:11; Isaiah 61:3).

Today, I invite you to plead the blood of Jesus over your life and take back everything the enemy has stolen from you! Remember the blood of Jesus will never lose its power because it's HIS BLOOD that will give you the overcoming power you need.

KEY PROMISE SCRIPTURE

"But he was wounded for our transgressions, he was bruised for our iniquities: the chastisement of our peace was upon him; and with his stripes we are healed"
(Isaiah 53:5 KJV)

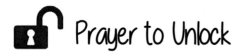 Prayer to Unlock

I thank You Jesus for the Blood You shed on Calvary. I plead the powerful Blood of Jesus all over me. I cleanse myself with the Blood of Jesus. The Blood washes away all of my sins, iniquities, and transgressions. I plead the Blood of Jesus over every organ in my body. The DNA in Your Blood is flowing through my veins. I will walk in the divine healing of Jesus' Blood that has restored my health. I plead the Blood of Jesus over my eyes: let me see You in everything I do. I plead the Blood of Jesus over my ears: let me hear Your voice. I plead the Blood of Jesus over my heart: heal it and give me a heart that is full of Your love. I plead the Blood of Jesus over my

hands: let everything I touch prosper and succeed. I plead the Blood of Jesus over my feet: let me walk in the dominion and authority You have given me. I plead the Blood of Jesus over my marriage, family, home, church, ministry, finances and anything else (list any other petition) _____. I thank You that the overcoming power in Your Blood brings me life. In Jesus' Name, Amen.

Declarations

I Decree and Declare that the Blood of Jesus is all over me.

I Decree and Declare I am an overcomer through the Blood of Jesus.

I Decree and Declare the Blood of Jesus has set me free and redeemed me.

I Decree and Declare the Blood of Jesus makes me healed and whole.

I Decree and Declare the Blood of Jesus gives me wonder-working power.

I Decree and Declare the Blood of Jesus still works and will never lose its power.

Key Points

"Write the vision and make it plain on tablets, that he may run who reads it."
(Habakkuk 2:2 NKJV)

Jot down any key points or key ideas you gained from this section...

Think About It: How can I apply these keys in my life?

_____
_____
_____
_____
_____
_____
_____
_____
_____
_____
_____
_____
_____
_____
_____
_____
_____
_____
_____
_____
_____
_____

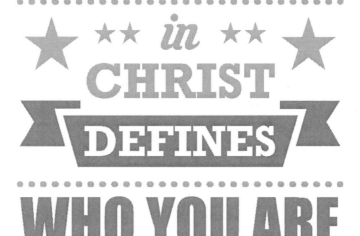

YOUR IDENTITY *in* CHRIST DEFINES WHO YOU ARE

Cindy Roopchand

9

YOUR TRUE IDENTITY
IN CHRIST

The ninth key to being an overcomer is to know your true identity in Christ. Once you become a born-again believer, the Bible states you become a new creature in Christ. Therefore, the former things have passed away and God is doing a new thing in you and through you. You are no longer who you used to be. The old you has passed away and the new you has come alive.

Your identity comes from what God says about you and what God has done for you. The Bible says in John 1:12-13: "Yet to all who did receive him, to those who believed in his name, he gave the right to become children of God – children born not of natural descent, nor of human decision or a husband's will, but born of God." This Scripture calls us children of God. We are sons and daughters of the Most High God.

Galatians 4:7 declares, "So you are no longer a slave, but God's child; and since you are his child, God has made you also an heir." This Scripture is telling us we are heirs of God and we inherit all of our spiritual riches and blessings because we belong to Him. As a spiritual Father, God will provide for and take care of you.

The enemy is an identity thief. He will do anything to stop you from knowing who you are. He wants to rob you of the truth. This is why he tries to consume you with the lies of this world. He wants to deceive and manipulate you into believing his lies. Everything he says contradicts the Word of God. This is why it is so powerful for you to know what the Word of God says about you, so you won't believe his lies.

The Bible calls him the father of lies, but Jesus is the Way, the Truth and the Life.

We have to stop thinking about what people are saying about us and start believing in what God says. When Jesus went to the cross and shed His blood for us, He gained a new inheritance for us. If someone wants to know who the father of a child is, they take a DNA or blood test. When we become born again believers, Jesus' blood is now part of our spiritual DNA. Let me introduce you to who you are in Christ. The Bible declares:

- You are God's beloved - Jeremiah 31:3.

- You are a child of God - 1 John 3:1

- You are healed – Isaiah 53:5

- You are whole - Colossians 2:10

- You are a co-heir with CHRIST- Romans 8:17

- You are forgiven - Psalm 103:12

- You are important - 1 Peter 2:9

- You are free - Galatians 5:1

- You are a new creature in Christ – 2 Corinthians 5:17

- You are protected – Psalm 121:3

- You are redeemed – Colossians 1:4

- You are fearfully and wonderfully made - Psalm 139:14

- You are not alone - Deuteronomy 31:8

- You are God's masterpiece- Ephesians 2:10

- You are loved – John 3:16

- You are blessed – Ephesians 1:3

- You are more than a Conqueror – Romans 8:37

- You are victorious - 1 John 5:3

- You are set apart and chosen- 1 Peter 2:9

- You are an overcomer - 1 John 5:4-5

- You are family - Ephesians 2:19

- You are strong – Psalm 68:35

- You are unique - Psalm 119:13

- You are bold - 2 Corinthians 3:12

- You are created for a purpose - Jeremiah 29:11

KEY PROMISE SCRIPTURE

"Yet to all who did receive him, to those who believed in his name, he gave the right to become children of God"
(John 1:12)

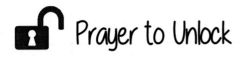 # Prayer to Unlock

Father God, we pray that we have a revelation of who we are in Your eyes. May we never believe the lies of the enemy that tell us otherwise. May we see ourselves the way You see us. May we confess with our mouth who You say we are:

> *"I am Your child" (See John 1:12).*

> *"I am chosen before the creation of the world" (See Ephesians 1:4, 11).*

> *"I am forgiven" (See Ephesians 1:7).*

> *"I am protected" (See John 10:28).*

> *"I am the righteousness of God" (See 2 Corinthians 5:21).*

> *"I am holy and blameless" (See Ephesians 1:4).*

> *"I have God's power" (See Ephesians 6:10).*

> *"I am victorious" (See 1 Corinthians 15:57).*

> *"I am an overcomer" (See 1 John 4:4).*

Thank You for the identity we have in You. In Jesus' Name, Amen.

Declarations

I Decree and Declare I am a child of the King - Galatians 3:26

I Decree and Declare I am a temple of the Holy Spirit-1 Corinthians 6:19

I Decree and Declare I am God's Masterpiece -Ephesians 2:10

I Decree and Declare I am Redeemed - Psalm 55:18

I Decree and Declare I am Fearfully and Wonderfully Made - Psalm 139:14

 Key Points

"Write the vision and make it plain on tablets, that he may run who reads it. "
(Habakkuk 2:2 NKJV)

Jot down any key points or key ideas you gained from this section...

Think About It: How can I apply these keys in my life?

_____
_____
_____
_____
_____
_____
_____
_____

PRAYER
PREPARES
the way

CINDY ROOPCHAND

10

PRAYERS MOVE
MOUNTAINS

The tenth key to being an overcomer is to know the power of prayer. If we want to be overcomers, we need to fight our battles on our knees. Prayer is a powerful tool every overcomer needs. It activates the power we need to overcome every problem or challenge we face in life. It is a spiritual weapon that has unlimited power. The discipline of prayer is essential for every believer because prayer connects us with God. It gives us the spiritual breath we need to survive and thrive. Prayer gives us triumph over every trial.

Prayer is basically having a conversation with God. He is our Heavenly Father. He knows what we need. This is why it is important to go to God with sincere prayers. We should be honest and transparent with Him and make our prayers personal. We can pray to God about anything. The list is endless. You can pray about your physical, emotional, financial, and spiritual needs. You can pray for others and any concerns you may have.

There is no right or wrong way to pray. However, the Bible does say that when we pray we should pray in faith. "And all things, whatsoever ye shall ask in prayer, believing, ye shall receive" (Matthew 21:22 KJV). We should also pray in the name of Jesus Christ because the Bible says, "And whatsoever ye shall ask in my name, that will I do, that the Father may be glorified in the Son. If ye shall ask anything in my name, I will do it" (John 14:13-14 KJV).

There is no set formula for prayer. Your prayers should come from your heart and be individualized to suit you. However, I will share some things I include during my prayer time with the Lord. During my prayer time, I dedicate some time for confession or repentance. We all make mistakes and fall short of God's glory every day. The Bible says that sin will hinder our prayers from being answered. "If I regard iniquity in my heart, the Lord will not hear me" (Psalm 66:18 KJV). "But your iniquities have separated between you and your God, and your sins have hid His face from you, that He will not hear" (Isaiah 59:2 KJV). Therefore, daily repentance is important because you don't want sin to affect your prayer and relationship with God.

I love to quote Psalm 51:10 (KJV): "Create in me a clean heart, O God; and renew a right spirit within me." I ask God to forgive me for any sins I have committed, the ones I am aware of, and to reveal the ones I am unaware of so I can repent.

I also believe during your prayer time you should include a form of thanksgiving. I believe praise and worship is a portal into God's presence. The Bible says, "Enter into his gates with thanksgiving, and into his courts with praise, be thankful unto him, and bless his name" (Psalm 100:4 KJV). So, I begin by thanking God for all that He has done for me and what He will do for me. I bless His name.

After I have confessed my sins and praised God with thanksgiving, I make my specific request to Him or I tell Him what I need Him to help me with. I even quote or find Scriptures that help me with my petitions. After that, I pray for others or intercede for them. Sometimes I will also pray in my prayer language or in the Holy Spirit like the Bible says in Jude 1:20 (NKJV): "But you beloved, building up yourself on your most holy faith, praying in the Holy Ghost." Then I end my prayer time with worship, praise and thanksgiving again.

The Bible says to "pray without ceasing" (1 Thessalonians 5:17 KJV). It is important to pray continuously, and to keep on praying until something happens. Do not give up. Sometimes God may not answer our prayers right away; but keep pressing on. God knows what's best for us, and prayer will align us with His purpose for our lives.

The Bible stresses the importance of prayer and commands us to seek the Lord in prayer:

"Seek the Lord and his strength, seek his face continually" (1 Chronicles 16:11 KJV).

"Seek the Lord while he may be found, call upon him while he is near" (Isaiah 55:6).

"The Lord is near unto all that call upon him, to all that call upon him in truth" (Psalm 145:18).

"Draw near to God and He will draw near to you" (James 4:8 NKJV).

"I will therefore that men pray everywhere, lifting up holy hands, without wrath and doubting" (1Timothy 2:8 KJV).

There are many examples in the Bible of men and women who prayed when they needed breakthroughs; they faced problems and wanted God to perform a miracle in their lives. I think of Hannah, for example, who was barren. Her powerful prayers resulted in the birth of her son, Samuel, one of the greatest prophets (See 1 Samuel 1:27). I also think of the prophetess, Anna, who prayed and was allowed to see the newborn Jesus, the Messiah, in her lifetime (See Luke 2:36-37). Daniel prayed three times a day, and God answered his prayers even when he faced death for defying the king's orders (Daniel 6:10). King David prayed morning, noon and night (Psalm 55:17).

The greatest example of a person who prayed in the Bible is Jesus. It was in the Garden of Gethsemane that we see Jesus fighting His battle on His knees through vehement prayer. This is how Jesus won the victory at Calvary. It was when He prayed, *"...not my will, but thine, be done. And there appeared an angel unto him from heaven, strengthening him. And being in an agony he prayed more earnestly: and his sweat was as it were great drops of blood falling down to the ground"* (Luke 22:42-44 KJV). Our prayers can release angels to strengthen us when we are weak.

In addition, the gospel of Mark says, "And in the morning, rising up a great while before day, he went out, and departed into a solitary place and there prayed" (Mark 1:35 KJV). "And it came to pass in those days, that He went out into the mountain to pray, and continued all night in prayer to God" (Luke 6:12 KJV). So, according to these Scriptures, Jesus prayed whether it was early in the morning or at night. Persistent prayer makes you an overcomer.

The enemy will do anything in his power to prevent us from praying. He wants us to focus on our problems rather than the God who is the answer to all our problems. The enemy also wants us to be so busy that we have no time to sit down and pray.

This is why it is critical that you set aside a special time every day to meet with God and pray. Please guard your prayer time and do not let anyone or anything interrupt you. I would suggest picking a time where you know there will be the least interruptions or distractions, maybe early in the morning or in the evening. Please make time daily to pray and please keep your appointment with your Heavenly Father. I know He looks forward to your one-on-one appointments together. Remember, prayer time is a non-negotiable item; it must happen for your breakthrough.

KEY PROMISE SCRIPTURE

"If my people, who are called by my name, will humble themselves, and pray and seek My face, and turn from their wicked ways, then will I hear from heaven, and will forgive their sin and heal their land"
(2 Chronicles 7:14 NKJV)

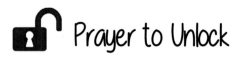 Prayer to Unlock

Heavenly Father, I will prioritize our time together. Your Word says, "And pray in the Spirit on all occasions with all kinds of prayers and requests. With this in mind, be alert and always keep on praying for all the Lord's people" (Ephesians 6:18). I will communicate with You daily. I will sit at Your feet, Jesus, and wait to hear from You. I will read Your Word and listen for Your will and instructions for my life. I will pray in Spirit and in Truth. Lord, You promise to answer whatever we may ask in

Jesus' name, according to Your will. Therefore, through my prayer time, I will seek Your will for my life. I will pray in the authority of Jesus Christ. And I will hold on to the promise that You gave in John 16:23-24: "Very truly, I tell you, My Father will give you whatever you ask in my name. Until now you have not asked for anything in my name. Ask and you will receive, and your joy will be complete."

Father, I ask that You lead and guide me all the days of my life, in Jesus' Name. Amen.

Declarations

I Decree and Declare I will make time to spend with my Heavenly Father.

I Decree and Declare I will prioritize my prayer time.

I Decree and Declare I will pray every day.

I Decree and Declare I will seek the will of God for my life during my prayer time.

I Decree and Declare I will pray in the name of Jesus Christ, for He holds the authority.

 Key Points

"Write the vision and make it plain on tablets, that he may run who reads it."
(Habakkuk 2:2 NKJV)

Jot down any key points or key ideas you gained from this section...

Think About It: How can I apply these keys in my life?

_____

_____

_____

_____

_____

_____

_____

_____

_____

_____

_____

_____

_____

_____

_____

_____

_____

_____

_____

_____

_____

_____

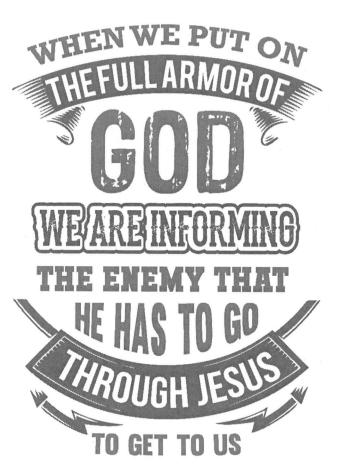

WHEN WE PUT ON THE FULL ARMOR OF GOD WE ARE INFORMING THE ENEMY THAT HE HAS TO GO THROUGH JESUS TO GET TO US

Cindy Roopchand

11

THE ARMOR OF GOD

The eleventh key to being an overcomer is to put on the armor of God. People may not realize it but we are in a battle zone, in a war between good and evil. There is an unseen battle happening in the spirit realm between God and the enemy. When you step into the water and give yourself to the Lord, you are drafted into God's army. However, do not be afraid because, when you submit your life to Jesus Christ, you are automatically on the winning side. We are soldiers of Jesus Christ, and we are commissioned to engage in battle. When you go into battle, you must be trained and prepared for victory.

The way to win this war is by listening to your commanding officer, Jesus. Every day the enemy is ready to attack us. He never takes the day off and is ready to come at us when we least expect it. We have to guard ourselves because the Bible says, "Stay alert! Watch out for your great enemy, the devil. He prowls around like a roaring lion, looking for someone to devour" (1 Peter 5:8 NLT). Remember, a solider never goes into a battlefield unprepared. When you are not prepared, you become an easy target for the enemy.

The Bible clearly shows us how to protect ourselves from the invisible enemy in Ephesians 6:11-18:

> Put on the full armor of God, so that you can take your stand against the devil's schemes. For our struggle is not against flesh and blood, but against the rulers, against the authorities, against the powers of this dark world and against the spiritual forces of evil in the heavenly realms. Therefore, put on the full armor of God, so that when the day of evil comes, you may be able to stand your

86

ground, and after you have done everything, to stand. Stand firm then, with the belt of truth buckled around your waist, with the breastplate of righteousness in place, and with your feet fitted with the readiness that comes from the gospel of peace. In addition to all this, take up the shield of faith, with which you can extinguish all the flaming arrows of the evil one. Take the helmet of salvation and the sword of the Spirit, which is the Word of God. And pray in the Spirit on all occasions with all kinds of prayers and requests. With this in mind, be alert and always keep on praying for all the Lord's people.

These scriptures clearly explain what we are commissioned to do and how to equip ourselves to do it. We are to put on the spiritual armor of God. This armor will help us to stand against the strategies of the enemy and to prevail against all his schemes to trap and deceive us. This will allow us to gain victory over his assaults and onslaughts. The spiritual armory will help us to overcome every attack. It will help us to break the strongholds and avoid the fiery darts of the enemy.

So, in order to survive the difficult trials and situations in our lives, we must be well protected by the whole armor of God. The armor of God is made up of six pieces of equipment or spiritual weapons. It's important that we don't just put on certain pieces of the armor but put on the **whole** armor of God, so we will not leave any opening in our lives for the enemy to penetrate. Five out of the six spiritual weapons are defensive weapons used to protect us. The last spiritual weapon is an offensive weapon, the Belt of Truth. The six weapons are: the belt of truth, the breastplate of righteousness, the shoes of the Gospel, the shield of faith, the helmet of salvation and the sword of the Spirit. The last spiritual weapon is an offensive weapon – the sword of the Spirit.

The Belt of Truth has been given to support, strengthen and protect us with the truth. I think of weight lifters, who wear a special belt to support their core area when they lift heavy weights. The Truth is your core being. When you know the truth about God, it protects you from the lies of the enemy. The enemy loves to manipulate and deceive us into believing his version of reality. Remember, Jesus is the Truth and the enemy is a liar. This is why it is important for us to know and study the Word of God so we will know the truth and the truth will set us free.

The Breastplate of Righteousness protects our heart and vital organs. Think of a police officer. They would not go out there without their bulletproof vest because it protects their heart. Your heart is your life. If you lose your heart, you will lose your life. God is telling us we need to guard our heart. Do not let lies, unforgiveness, bitterness, and anger contaminate your heart. You should have the heart of Jesus. Remember, righteousness is not from ourselves but from Jesus. We can stand before Him because of what He did for us on the cross.

As soldiers of God, we are marching into a battle and we need to have our boots ready to deliver the Gospel of peace. We need to ensure we have shoes that are strong, secure, and won't allow us to slip and fall. When we are prepared and skilled in the Gospel, we are protected from the schemes of the enemy, which try to cause us to fall. We need to have shoes that will allow us to follow the leadership of the Lord. We need to go where the Lord leads and guides us. As Christians, we need to walk in His peace and truth. We have to march and spread the Gospel. We need God's peace to spread the Good News. God is our peace; He gives us the Peace that surpasses all understanding. The enemy wants to steal our peace, which is why we need to be constantly with the Prince of Peace. We need to walk in His peace, share the Good News, and be light in this dark world.

The next piece of armory is the Shield of Faith. It helps us to "extinguish all the flaming darts of the evil one." This protects us from the enemy's weapons, attacks, and darts. The shield of faith covers us in all directions. The enemy's attacks can sometimes cause us to walk in unbelief and doubt. However, faith is the choice to believe God regardless of what the situation looks like. God wants us to walk by faith and not by sight. When we know the truth, the Word of God, then we begin to walk by faith. Once we choose faith over fear, we become overcomers.

The Helmet of Salvation was created to protect our minds. Remember when they put the crown of thorns on Jesus' head on Calvary? He was redeeming our peace of mind. We want our minds to be guarded by the Lord. It protects our thinking process. God wants us to have a sound mind, which is why the enemy tries to bring confusion and doubt into our lives. Joyce Meyer says, "The battlefield is in your mind." If the enemy has our mind, he knows he can have our life. The mind is what God uses to give us insight and creative power to help us walk in our purpose and calling. This is why the enemy is trying to pollute our mind. He is a deceiver and, if you do not know the truth, you will begin to believe his lies. The Bible tells us to renew our minds daily. To do so, it is crucial for us to stay in the Word of God, so we have the mind of God. When we have the mind of Christ, we will be confident in our salvation and in the promises of God.

The only offensive weapon in the Armor of God is the Sword of the Spirit, the Word of God. This is the weapon we use to fight the enemy back. The Word of God is powerful. Hebrews 4:12 (NLT) states, "For the word of God is alive and powerful. It is sharper than the sharpest two-edged sword, cutting between soul and spirit, between joint and marrow. It exposes our innermost thoughts and desires." Jesus Christ used the Sword of the Spirit to fight and defeat the enemy when He faced temptation by saying, "It is written…" (Matthew 4:4,6,7,10). If Jesus used the Word of God as His weapon to fight the enemy, then we need to use the Word of God, too.

It is essential for you to study and know the Word of God. When the enemy begins to attack you with his lies, you begin to fight him back with the scriptures. The Bible says the weapons of our warfare are not carnal but mighty through the pulling down of strongholds (See 2 Corinthians 10:4). We cannot fight these battles with our fists. We need to fight these battles on our knees through prayer and through the Word of God.

The Bible declares Jesus won the war and the enemy is already defeated. However, because we live in a fallen world until Jesus comes back, the enemy is still on the prowl. The Armor of God guards your mind and heart. Just as you get physically dressed in the morning, please make sure you are spiritually dressed. These spiritual weapons the Lord has given us will equip us to be overcomers and victors. When we study and apply them to our lives daily, we can be more than conquerors and defeat what was trying to defeat us.

KEY PROMISE SCRIPTURE

"Put on the full armor of God, so that you can take your stand against the devil's schemes. For our struggle is not against flesh and blood, but against the rulers, against the authorities, against the powers of this dark world and against the spiritual forces of evil in the heavenly realms. Therefore, put on the full armor of God, so that when the day of evil comes, you may be able to stand your ground, and after you have done everything, to stand. Stand firm then, with the belt of truth buckled around your waist, with the breastplate of righteousness in place, and with your feet fitted with the readiness that comes from the gospel of peace. In addition to all this, take up the shield of faith, with which you can extinguish all the flaming arrows of the evil one. Take the helmet of salvation and the sword of the Spirit, which is the word of God. And pray in the Spirit on all occasions with all kinds of prayers and requests. With this in mind, be alert and always keep on praying for all the Lord's people"
(Ephesians 6:11-18)

🔓 Prayer to Unlock

Lord, help me today to put on the whole armor of God so that I may stand against the attacks of the enemy. For I know the enemy is roaming around like a lion seeking whom he may devour. Give me Your discernment to recognize the attacks of the enemy and to use my spiritual weapons to fight and defeat him.

Let me put on the Belt of Truth and know that You are the way, the truth, and the life. Today I stand on Your Truth, which is the Word of God and not on the lies of the enemy.

Today I put on the Breastplate of Righteousness, my bulletproof vest, and I will not allow the darts of the enemy to pierce me. I know that I am in right standing with You because of what Jesus did for me at Calvary. Today, I will guard my heart because I know that God loves me, and I will love others.

Today I put on my spiritual shoes and I will walk in the path of peace because You are the Prince of Peace. I put on my Shoes of the Gospel and I will share the good news with someone today.

Today I take the Shield of Faith and I will walk by faith and not by sight. I bind fear, doubt, and unbelief, and I loose faith right now, in Jesus' name.

I put on my Helmet of Salvation and I cover my mind with Your truth and with Your blood. I know that today I will have the mind of Christ. Thank You for downloading your creative ideas, insights and revelation into my life.

Last of all, I take up the Sword of the Spirit, the Word of God, and I will use it when the enemy tries to tempt me. I will say, "It is written, That man shall not live by bread alone, but by every word of God" (Luke 4:4 KJV). I thank You, Jesus, for fighting my battles and defeating the enemy. Help me to be victorious and an overcomer like You. In Jesus' Name I ask these things. Amen.

Declarations

I Decree and Declare that I will put on the full armor of God.

I Decree and Declare that I will not be blindsided by the attacks of the enemy.

I Decree and Declare that no weapon formed against me shall prosper today.

I Decree and Declare I will use my spiritual weapons to defeat the enemy.

I Decree and Declare I will use the Sword of the Spirit and my tongue will confess the Word of God.

 Key Points

"Write the vision and make it plain on tablets, that he may run who reads it."
(Habakkuk 2:2 NKJV)

Jot down any key points or key ideas you gained from this section...

Think About It: How can I apply these keys in my life?

_____

_____

_____

_____

_____

_____

_____

_____

_____

_____

_____

_____

_____

_____

_____

_____

_____

_____

_____

YOUR
WORDS
— *Hold* —
GREAT POWER
Use them
WISELY

Cindy Roopchand

12

SPEAK LIFE, NOT DEATH

The twelfth key to being an overcomer is to speak life over every situation. When you speak life, you are speaking God's Word over your circumstances. The Bible says, "Death and Life are in the power of the tongue" (Proverbs 18:21 KJV). Our words can help or hurt people. When God comes into our lives, He wants to use our tongue. Our tongue is how we communicate with one another. Sometimes people do not realize the power they have, specifically, through their tongue.

The tongue is a small part of the body, yet it can have the greatest impact. The Book of James states, "Likewise, the tongue is a small part of the body, but it makes great boasts. Consider that a great forest is set on fire by a small spark. The tongue also is a fire, a world of evil among the parts of the body. It corrupts the whole body, sets the whole course of one's life on fire, and is itself set on fire by hell. All kinds of animals, birds, reptiles and sea creatures are being tamed and have been tamed by mankind, but no human being can tame the tongue. It is a restless evil, full of deadly poison" (James 3:5-8). You can see from the above Scripture the power the tongue has and the untold damage it can do if it is untamed. It is important to ask God to tame your tongue and help you control it. This is ultimately something only God can do. This is why we need to surrender our tongue to Him.

The Book of Proverbs is the book of wisdom in the Bible. This book mentions the tongue over 150 times. I believe this is teaching us the importance of using our words wisely. We need to be mindful before we speak because we are called to be oracles and mouthpieces for the Lord. We cannot do this if we have not surrendered our mouth and tongue to the Lord.

It is therefore important to use your tongue to glorify God and not to hurt others. You tongue should be used to praise God. It was not created to speak defeat, to gossip, to curse, to criticize, or to hurt others. Rather, your tongue was created to speak life, to speak victory, to speak truth, to build people up, to encourage and compliment them. God desires to use our tongue to further the Gospel to bless others. The Bible says, "Anxiety weighs down a man, but a kind word can cheer him up" (Proverbs 12:25).

It is important to speak the truth and not lies, for God is Truth. The Bible says in John 14:6 that Jesus is the way, the truth and the life. The enemy is a liar. "He was a murderer from the beginning, not holding to the truth, for there is no truth in him. When he lies, he speaks his native language, for he is a liar and the father of lies" (John 8:44). Remember, when you use your tongue to speak truth and then lie, you have a forked tongue just like the serpent, the enemy. You don't want the enemy controlling your mouth; you want God to.

So much power is released when we speak. Remember God spoke the heavens and the earth into existence. Since our body responds to words, it is critical that we speak life even over dead situations. We should speak in truth and the Word of God is Truth. Facts may be the circumstances we are facing. However, truth is greater than facts. It may be a fact that I am going through a difficult situation; however, the truth is I am going to overcome this situation.

Remember, storms and mountains are the problems we are facing, which may include a sickness, marital issues, loss of a loved one etc. It is important to speak to our storms and tell them we are coming out wiser and better. We need to speak to our mountains and command them to be removed, in Jesus' name. We need to confess and declare out loud with our mouths that we are an overcomer. We are more than a conqueror. We can do all things through Christ who strengthens us.

Complaining and murmuring can only hold back our breakthroughs and cause us to be stuck in our situation. Complaining is releasing negative faith. When you complain, it's as if you are cursing God and saying His provision is not good enough.

There are so many stories in the Bible that demonstrate how murmuring and complaining bring negative results. Think about the Israelites in the Old Testament, how they complained about their hardships instead of praying to God. As a result, many of them were destroyed when God sent a plague of fire to punish them. In addition, the Israelites complained about the lack of meat in the wilderness. They were lusting after the things they did not have. God then sent quails but, as the people began to eat them, He struck them with a plague that killed many.

Also, the Israelites were complaining about being stuck in the wilderness facing the giants in the Promised Land and wishing to return to Egypt. This showed their rebellion against God's leaders, and their failure to trust in His Promises. Due to their complaints, they were not allowed to enter the Promised Land, so they wandered in the wilderness until they died.

These Bible stories show us the disastrous consequences of complaining and murmuring. We do not want to block our blessings and breakthroughs because of our murmuring and complaining. Let's shut the door to speaking defeat and open our mouth to speaking life. Remember, our words have power and can help us to be victorious.

There is tremendous power when we use our tongue to speak the Word of God and agree with God's Word. The Bible declares that every time we speak God's Word, the angels hear it and they hearken to the voice of His Word; they hasten to carry out that word and bring it to pass (See Psalm 103:20).

When you are in right standing with God, you can speak the Word of God and it can come to pass. The Bible says in Job 22:28 you can declare and decree a thing and it will be established in your life. God is watching over His Word to perform it (See Jeremiah 1:12). Isaiah 55:11 says, His Word will not return to Him void. The Bible states that on judgment day we will all have to give an account of every idle or careless word we have spoken (See Matthew 12:36).

KEY PROMISE SCRIPTURE

"Death and life are in the power of the tongue *to "*
(Proverbs 18:21 KJV)

🔓 Prayer to Unlock

Today in Jesus' name I will use my tongue to speak life and not death. I plead the blood of Jesus over my tongue and will use it to glorify God and others. I will bless the Lord at all times. My tongue will be used to help people and not hurt them. I will use my tongue to speak encouragement. I will use my tongue as a sword of the Spirit and confess the Word of God. My tongue will bless and not curse. It will be used to glorify the Lord and to spread the message of hope. My tongue will be used as a powerful weapon to defeat the kingdom of darkness. I submit my tongue to You, Lord; let my words be used by You. I ask these things in Jesus' Name. Amen.

Declarations

I Decree and Declare that I will speak life today.

I Decree and Declare that I will speak truth.

I Decree and Declare that I will speak victory today.

I Decree and Declare that I will use my mouth to bless and encourage others.

I Decree and Declare that no longer will I complain or murmur.

 Key Points

"Write the vision and make it plain on tablets, that he may run who reads it. "
(Habakkuk 2:2 NKJV)

Jot down any key points or key ideas you gained from this section...

Think About It: How can I apply these keys in my life?

_____

_____

_____

_____

_____

_____

_____

_____

_____

_____

_____

_____

_____

_____

_____

_____

_____

_____

_____

_____

Fasting
IS THE
— ROAD —
THAT LEADS TO
BREAKTHROUGHS
— IN THE —
Spirit

Cindy Roopchand

13

FASTING FOR
BREAKTHROUGHS

The thirteenth key to being an overcomer is fasting. When we fast, we are denying our flesh or our earthly desires. Fasting allows God to have His way. Fasting brings breakthroughs, revivals and miracles. It is about self-denial and allowing God to flow through us. Fasting is also about obedience. It is a powerful tool that we use to help us become overcomers.

Many Biblical leaders fasted. Esther fasted for the people of Israel, Moses fasted, Daniel fasted, and Jesus fasted. When you are fasting, you need to have the right spirit and the right motives. Fasting is not a way to manipulate God or earn brownie points. Rather, it is a way to submit to God, to connect with Him and hear from Him. It is a way to gain direction about God's will in your life.

Fasting can be an individual or private decision, or a corporate one. Corporate fasting can be powerful especially when people pray together because there is power in agreement (See Matthew 18:19).

We can fast in the way we choose. How long you decide to fast is a decision between you and God. In the Bible, Daniel fasted for twenty-one days, Jesus and Moses fasted for forty days and Esther fasted for three days without food and water. Esther needed a breakthrough, when she found out Haman was trying to exterminate the Jews. Esther asked the Jews to fast with her because she needed to hear from God. She needed His wisdom and courage to know what to do. After three days, she prepared a banquet where she was wise and brave enough to expose the plans of Haman and to entreat the King to spare her people.

Fasting makes you brave and courageous. It allows God's Spirit to work through you and speak through you. Fasting helps you to make Godly decisions when you are at a crossroads in your life. When you deny your flesh, you allow God's Spirit to fully take over from you and powerful things can happen.

There is a story in Matthew chapter 17 about the disciples encountering an epileptic boy possessed by a demon, which they couldn't cast out. They asked Jesus why they could not cast out this demon. He said it was because of their unbelief and added that these types can only come out through fasting and prayer. Fasting helps you overcome your unbelief. If there are certain areas in your life where you need a breakthrough, then fasting will help you. Sometimes you have to turn your plate down and deny your flesh.

Certain situations in our lives can make us self-absorbed and we forget to become God-absorbed. Fasting brings humility and removes any pride from us. It allows us to see we need God to help us through some of our storms. God looks at our motives and at our hearts when we decide to fast. When you are fasting, you should replace a meal with spiritual food, which is the Word of God.

Fasting is not the same as dieting and there are different types of fast. There is a full fast, which means no food at all. Jesus and Moses did this type of fast where they went without any food or water for forty days. The Bible also shares about the Daniel fast. This is a partial fast when you give up some pleasurable food. For example, Daniel did not eat meat or drink wine.

There is also a fast where you remove pleasurable activities, for example, no television or social media. In addition, it shares in the Bible, that when married couples were fasting, they would refrain from certain pleasurable activities as well.

It is important therefore if you are doing a fast that you remove a pleasurable meal or activities. You should select something that demonstrates a big sacrifice from you. It should be something that you love or desire that you are willing to give up to show God that you love Him more. You want to show God that you want to move in the Spirit and bring it into the natural.

When you make the decision to fast, you can expect some resistance from the enemy. However, do not allow this to stop you from fasting. The Bible demonstrates this when Jesus was fasting because the enemy came to tempt Him three times. Fasting can make us weak and vulnerable in the natural, but in the end, it will make you stronger in the spirit. Jesus fought the enemy's temptation with the Word of God: that was His spiritual food and weapon.

It is important to fear God and not the enemy. It is crucial for us to know the Word of God and study it especially during a period of fasting or when you are consecrating yourself to God. The enemy knows that when we fast, pray, and study the Word of God, we are going to have power. Remember, the Holy Spirit within you is greater than the enemy, and the benefits of fasting will far outweigh his temptations.

When you are fasting, the Bible says you should do it in secret (See Matthew 6:18). When you do it in secret, God will reward you openly or publicly. When you fast, it should be something between you and God, not something you do to seem high and holy in front of other people.

In addition, be purposeful when you are going too fast. I usually pray about what I should fast about and then I take it to God. For example, if I am fasting for healing, I would write it down, pray about it, look up scriptures about it and begin to declare these scriptures over my life. Remember, fasting is about changing you and not about changing God. It is about submitting yourself to God's will and purpose for your life.

To conclude, fasting is about drawing close to the Lord and gaining His strength. Fasting is a choice and, if done with the right intentions, it can lead to many breakthroughs in your life. Pray and ask God if you need to do a fast. If you do, consider which type of fast you would like to do that will honor God. Fasting will lead you to be an overcomer.

KEY PROMISE SCRIPTURE

"'Even now,' declares the Lord, 'return to me with all your heart, with fasting and weeping and mourning"
(Joel 2:12)

 # Prayer to Unlock

I know fasting is a choice. I pray in Jesus' name, if it is God's will for me to fast, that He will reveal it to me. I pray that I will be obedient and fast when I am supposed to. I pray that I will have the desire to fast and make it part of my lifestyle. I pray during my fast that I will draw near to the Lord, and that I will spend time with Him and read His Word. I thank You, God, that during my time of fasting I will hear from You and You will guide me in the right path. I thank You, God, that my fasting will bring results and breakthroughs. In Jesus' name I ask these things. Amen

Declarations

I Decree and Declare that I will draw near to the Lord by fasting and praying.

I Decree and Declare that fasting will bring breakthroughs in my life.

I Decree and Declare that when I fast, I will discover the will of God for my life.

I Decree and Declare that I will be purposeful and prayerful when I am fasting.

I Decree and Declare that I will make fasting a part of my lifestyle.

 Key Points

"Write the vision and make it plain on tablets, that he may run who reads it."
(Habakkuk 2:2 NKJV)

Jot down any key points or key ideas you gained from this section...

Think About It: How can I apply these keys in my life?

_____
_____
_____
_____
_____
_____
_____
_____
_____
_____
_____
_____
_____
_____
_____
_____
_____
_____
_____
_____
_____

PRAISE AND WORSHIP ALLOW US TO ENTER THE GATEWAYS OF HEAVEN

CINDY ROOPCHAND

14

PRAISE AND WORSHIP

The fourteenth key to becoming an overcomer is praise and worship. Praise and worship are crucial elements because they release power. They take us into the glorious presence and power of God. The Bible states that God inhabits the praises of His people (See Psalm 22:3). God loves to dwell with His people especially when we are praising and worshiping Him. Praise and worship takes our focus off our situations and puts it on our God. It allows us to magnify our God and not our circumstances.

The Bible says in the Book of Revelation that when we go to heaven, we will be singing praises and worshiping our Heavenly Father for all eternity. When we praise and worship God, it is like being connected to a spiritual IV. It keeps you going when you feel drained. When you want to give up, it gives you the boost you need to keep going. Praise and worship are expressions of our faith and they move God to dwell among us.

We are called to worship God. The Bible says, "Oh come, let us worship and bow down; let us kneel before the Lord, our Maker" (Psalm 95:6 ESV). "It is written, you shall worship the Lord your God, and him only shall you serve" (Luke 4:8 ESV). "But the hour is coming, and is now here, when true worshippers will worship the Father in spirit and truth, for the Father is seeking such people" (John 4:23 ESV).

There is a difference between praise and worship. Worship is when you are bragging about who God is. This is when you are focusing on all the attributes or dimensions of God. For example, He is the Creator of the Universe, He is the King of Kings, He is The Lord of Lords, He is My Healer, He is My Provider, He is My Protector, and He is the Great I AM,

He is whoever you need Him to be (refer to the list of Names or Attributes of God). We should worship God for who He is. When we worship God, it gives us a revelation of who He is. It gives us a heavenly or eternal perspective. It shifts our mindset from the natural to the supernatural.

The Bible commands us to praise the Lord. "Praise the Lord, all people on earth, praise his glory and might" (Psalm 96:7 GNT). "We proclaim how great you are and tell of the wonderful things you have done" (Psalm 75:1 GNT). "Praise him - he is your God, and you have seen with your own eyes the great and astounding things that he has done for you" (Deuteronomy 10:21 GNT).

Praise is thanking God for everything He has done in your life. Thank Him for saving you, delivering you, blessing you and keeping you. The list is endless for all the things we should be thanking the Lord for. We should thank God for the ability to walk, to talk, to be alive, and to have food on our table. These are things we may take for granted but someone might not have these blessings or privileges.

The Bible says, "Enter his gates with thanksgiving and his courts with praise; give thanks to him and praise His name" (Psalm 100:4). "Praise the Lord. Give thanks to the Lord, for he is good, his love endures forever" (Psalm 106:1). "I will extol the LORD at all times; his praise will always be on my lips" (Psalm 34:1). "Let all that I am praise the LORD; with my whole heart. I will praise his holy name. Let all that I am praise the Lord; may I never forget the good things he does for me. He forgives all my sins and heals all my diseases. He redeems me from death and crowns me with love and tender mercies" (Psalm 103:1-5 NLT).

Praise should be part of our lifestyle because the Bible says, "I will bless the Lord at all times, his praise shall continually be in my mouth" (Psalm 34:1 KJV). Praise and Worship opens the door to the spiritual realm. They transport us into God's presence and power. Praise and worship inject God's peace and joy into our life.

The Bible gives us different Biblical expressions of praise. Singing praise songs (See Psalm 9:11), clapping hands and shouting (See Psalm 47:1), with musical instruments and dancing (See Psalm 150:4), lifting up our hands (See Psalm 134:2), making a joyful noise (See Psalm 98:4) and "psalms and hymns and spiritual songs" (Ephesians 5:19-20 KJV).

I believe praise confuses the enemy. The enemy wants to defeat you and make you give up. He hates it when you praise God because he knows the power it holds. The Bible says, "By him therefore let us offer the sacrifice of praise to God continually, that is, the fruit of our lips giving thanks to his name" (Hebrews 13:15 KJV). This scripture reminds us that we should praise God regardless of our feelings or situation. In order to be victorious, we need to praise our way out of circumstances. When we praise and worship, we are surrendering all of our problems to God and allowing Him to take over.

In order to be an overcomer, we need to be worshiping warriors. The Tribe of Judah were victorious because they praised God and He fought their battles. Judah, in fact, means praise. Revelation 5:5 refers to Jesus as the "Lion of the tribe of Judah." Jesus is fighting our battles for us and all we have to do is praise Him in advance for the victory. God will do anything but fail you. Praise and Worship Him for the great things He has done and will do in your life.

███████████████████████

KEY PROMISE SCRIPTURE

"Let everything that has breath praise the LORD"
(Psalm 150:6)

🔓 Prayer to Unlock

With my whole heart I praise and adore You, Lord. I will praise You all the days of my life. Thank You, Lord, for giving me breath. I thank You for another day of life. I thank You for Your mercy and grace. Today, I will offer You the sacrifice of praise for the mighty works You have done in my life. I will worship You in Spirit and in Truth. Great is the Lord who is worthy to be praised! I will worship and adore You for who You are, my King, My Messiah, My High Priest, My Redeemer, My Protector, and My Rescuer. You are omniscient: You know all things. You are omnipresent, everywhere at all times. I bow down in Your presence and glorify You. For I know praise and worship will usher me into the Heavenly realm where I will encounter Your powerful presence. Your praises will continuously be in my mouth all the days of my life. I ask these things in Jesus' name. Amen.

Declarations

I Decree and Declare that I will praise the Lord as long as I have breath in my body.

I Decree and Declare that I will praise my way out.

I Decree and Declare that praise and worship is a portal into God's presence.

I Decree and Declare that I will be a worshiper.

I Decree and Declare My worship will help me win the war.

 Key Points

"Write the vision and make it plain on tablets, that he may run who reads it."
(Habakkuk 2:2 NKJV)

Jot down any key points or key ideas you gained from this section...

Think About It: How can I apply these keys in my life?

_____
_____
_____
_____
_____
_____
_____
_____

GATHERING

TOGETHER

Gives You

STRENGTH

AND

Strategies

CINDY ROOPCHAND

15

GATHERING TOGETHER/ FELLOWSHIP

The fifteenth key to becoming an overcomer is gathering together in fellowship with your sisters and brothers in Christ. The Bible says in Hebrews 10:25 (KJV), "Not forsaking the assembling of ourselves together …" There is power in unity and agreement when you gather together and uplift each other. When you are in fellowship, you encourage and motivate each other. Gathering together equips us and empowers us to do all that God has called us to do. It is important to build yourself up and have edifying conversations with others.

I believe it is imperative for you to get involved in the church. The church should be like a spiritual mother; it's a place where you should get fed spiritually and where you are nurtured to grow in your calling. I call my church my spiritual hospital because it is a place I can go to when I need to be revived, get my life back and recover from this journey called life. I also call my church, my gas station because I go there to get refueled or pumped up. I have to be honest. At times life is difficult; there are a lot of challenges being thrown at you and you feel discouraged and want to give up. However, when you get around your body of believers or the church, you get encouraged, you get strength, you get powered and you are able to get back up again and move into that the call that God has for you.

Church should be a support system. The enemy loves isolation because that's when he can prey on you. It is easier to defeat someone when they are walking by themselves versus when they are walking with others. It is harder for the enemy to defeat you because together you are stronger to fend off his attacks. There is power in numbers.

The Bible says faith comes by hearing and hearing the word of God. When you go to church, it is for instruction to teach you about God. Also, fellowship allows you to corporately worship and praise together. A lot of times people just go to church to receive, but I believe we should also go to church to give. We should give honor to God; we should give glory to Him. We should bring our worship, praises and thanksgiving to Him. The church is not only for you to go and get saved but it is also a place for the saved or born-again believers. When you fellowship with others, it should be a time where you remind each other of the promises of God.

The Bible warns us, as we approach the End Times that there will be much tribulation and difficulty. When those times of difficulty come, this is when we need to be in the church. The enemy is going to try to attack the children of God, but we should not fear because God is fighting for us. When the world gets darker, I believe the church will get brighter. God's strength will fall upon us and we will be able to defeat the enemy.

There is power when we walk in the unity and agreement of the Lord. The Bible says, "For where two or three gather in my name, there am I with them" (Matthew 18:20). God is in the midst of us when we gather together and lift up His name. When we worship God corporately signs, wonders, and miracles take place because He loves when we praise and worship Him. The Bible says, we were created to worship Jesus in Spirit and in Truth.

I encourage you to at least once a week find a way to fellowship with others whether in person or on the phone through prayer. Also, don't forsake the gathering of ourselves with the Lord in a corporate setting like the church. God did not create us to walk this life alone. We need God and to be around others. I think of the cross being both vertical and horizontal. I believe first, we need that vertical relationship with the Lord; then we can have a horizontal relationship with others sharing the love of God with them. When you share about your relationship with Jesus, that is when you are further equipped and encouraged in your journey.

Jesus left us with two commandments: to love God and to love our neighbors. The enemy hates when you fellowship because he knows someone might bring up a scripture to remind you of who you are in Christ. He knows the power we have when we gather together. Another reason why the enemy will try to discourage you from having a conversation with another believer or from going to church is because he knows we strengthen each other. This is why he deceives many into thinking they don't need to be around other believers of God, or they can just serve God by themselves. It is a trick from the enemy to rob you of the power of God.

The Bible says "...iron sharpens iron..." (Proverbs 27:17). When we meet together, we sharpen and equip one another for greater works. You can have fellowship gatherings anywhere, for example, at the park, in a coffee shop, at a restaurant. Remember, we bring the church, so don't only go to church but be the church. God loves to dwell in the House of the Lord, the church. Remember when Jesus walked this earth, He went to the temple. If Jesus went into the House of the Lord, so can we. Notice that Jesus seldom walked alone while He did His ministry on earth. He always had His disciples around Him. We shouldn't walk alone either.

KEY PROMISE SCRIPTURE

"Not forsaking the assembling of ourselves together..."
(Hebrews 10:25 KJV)

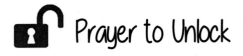 Prayer to Unlock

Thank You, Heavenly Father, for giving me my brothers and sisters in Christ to encourage, and to equip me to be all that You have called me to do. Thank You, Jesus, for the Church. Lead me to the right House of Worship. Let it be a place where they will teach the full truth about Yourself and a place where they will edify the Body of Christ. Let it be a place where You dwell like Zion, where people will know that God manifests because of the Fire and the Glory of God. I pray when we gather together that You will release Your power upon us so that we will see signs, wonders, and miracles. I pray, God, that You will bring the right people into my life that impact and inspire me to walk in my purpose. I thank You, Jesus, for Divine Connections and Divine Relationships.

Declarations

I Decree and Declare that I will not forsake the assembly of God.

I Decree and Declare that I will fellowship with others at least once a week.

I Decree and Declare that I will get around other believers of God, so we can empower and equip each other.

I Decree and Declare I will have Divine Connections and Relationships.

I Decree and Declare that I will pour into others and others will pour into me.

I Decree and Declare that I will be encouraged and inspired to do all that God called me to do.

 Key Points

"Write the vision and make it plain on tablets, that he may run who reads it. "
(Habakkuk 2:2 NKJV)

Jot down any key points or key ideas you gained from this section...

Think About It: How can I apply these keys in my life?

_____

_____

_____

_____

YOUR SPIRITUAL AUTHORITY ALLOWS YOU (to) VICTORIOUSLY WALK into your DESTINY

Cindy Roopchand

16

KNOW YOUR AUTHORITY

The sixteenth key to becoming an overcomer is to know your spiritual authority in Christ. According to Dictionary.com the word authority means "the power or right to give orders, make decisions, and enforce obedience." Therefore, spiritual authority is our right to use God's power to enforce the Word of God. As born-again believers, we have the permission to use the name of Jesus Christ. The Bible says, in Matthew 28:18, *"Then Jesus came to them and said, 'All authority in heaven and on earth has been given to me.'"* When we exercise the authority Jesus has given us, we have overcoming power.

The Scripture tells us, in Luke 9:1, "When Jesus had called the Twelve together, he gave them power and authority to drive out all demons and to cure diseases." He gave them supernatural power and protection: "I have given you authority to trample on snakes and scorpions and to overcome all the power of the enemy; nothing will harm you" (Luke 10:19). Jesus has given us the same authority to cast out demons, sicknesses and diseases. It is important for us to walk in this authority by using our mouths to command unclean spirits out of our lives. There is supernatural power in our words, so it is crucial for us to confess the Word of God as we cast out these spirits.

Your authority is accessed through faith in Jesus. You must believe in the authority that Jesus has given you. The Bible shares a story about deliverance in Mark 9:17-29 (NKJV).

Then one of the crowd answered and said, "Teacher, I brought You my son, who has a mute spirit. And wherever it seizes him, it throws him down; he foams at the mouth, gnashes his teeth,

132

and becomes rigid. So I spoke to Your disciples, that they should cast it out, but they could not." He answered him and said, "O faithless generation, how long shall I be with you? How long shall I bear with you? Bring him to Me." Then they brought him to Him. And when he saw Him, immediately the spirit convulsed him, and he fell on the ground and wallowed, foaming at the mouth. So He asked his father, "How long has this been happening to him?" And he said, "From childhood. And often he has thrown him both into the fire and into the water to destroy him. But if You can do anything, have compassion on us and help us." Jesus said to him, "If you can believe, all things are possible to him who believes." Immediately the father of the child cried out and said with tears, "Lord, I believe; help my unbelief!" When Jesus saw that the people came running together, He rebuked the unclean spirit, saying to it, "Deaf and dumb spirit, I command you, come out of him and enter him no more!" [26]Then the spirit cried out, convulsed him greatly, and came out of him. And he became as one dead, so that many said, "He is dead." But Jesus took him by the hand and lifted him up, and he arose. And when He had come into the house, His disciples asked Him privately, "Why could we not cast it out?" So He said to them, "This kind can come out by nothing but prayer and fasting."

Because the disciples lacked faith, they could not cast out the spirit from the boy. Faith is heaven's currency. It is how things move in the spirit. Remember we operate by our faith, not our feelings. We have to know that power and authority is given to those who believe in Him. When we believe, we shall receive.

The Bible tells us the authority is only given in **Jesus' name,** the name above all names. All things will bow to that name. "And these signs will accompany those who believe: In my name they will drive out demons; they will speak in new tongues; they will pick up snakes with their hands; and when they drink deadly poison, it will not hurt them at all; they will place their hands on sick people, and they will get well" (Mark 16:17-18).

The seventy-two returned with joy and said, *"Lord, even the demons submit to us in **your name"*** (Luke 10:17). And Peter said to the lame man, "Silver or gold I do not have, but what I do have I give you. *In the name of Jesus Christ* of Nazareth, walk"* (Acts 3:6).

If you want to operate in your God-given authority you must also spend time with the Lord. You have to read His Word and know His voice. The Bible says, faith comes by hearing the Word of God. Praying and fasting can also help you operate in the authority God has given us through Jesus.

Remember, authority is our legal right to use the power supplied by God. The Blood of Jesus, the name of Jesus and the Holy Spirit allow us to access the power of GOD. We have the authority to heal the sick, cast out demons, and stop the works of darkness, through Jesus Christ. Today, take authority over your situation and command things to change, in Jesus' Name. I pray that you will gain this revelation and walk in the authority of God.

KEY PROMISE SCRIPTURE

"Look, I have given you authority over all the power of the enemy, and you can walk among snakes and scorpions and crush them. Nothing will injure you"
(Luke 10:19 NLT)

🔓 Prayer to Unlock

Heavenly Father, I know as a believer, I have the authority to use the name of Jesus. I know that Name will gain all of heaven's attention. "Therefore God also has highly exalted Him, and given Him the name which is above every name, that at the name of Jesus every knee should bow, of things in heaven, and things in earth, and things under the earth" (Philippians 2:9-10 NKJV). In Jesus' Name, I use my authority to "tread on serpents and scorpions, and over all the power of the enemy" (Luke 10:19). Today I will walk in the authority Jesus gave me. The name of Jesus holds the power and the authority I need to be the overcomer God called me to be. I claim it now, in Jesus' name. Amen.

Declarations

I Decree and Declare that I will have a revelation of the authority I have as a believer of Jesus Christ.

I Decree and Declare that I have authority through Jesus Christ.

I Decree and Declare that I will walk in my God- Given Authority.

I Decree and Declare that I will have power over the enemy through Jesus Christ.

 Key Points

"Write the vision and make it plain on tablets, that he may run who reads it."
(Habakkuk 2:2 NKJV)

Jot down any key points or key ideas you gained from this section...

Think About It: How can I apply these keys in my life?

_____

_____

_____

_____

_____

_____

_____

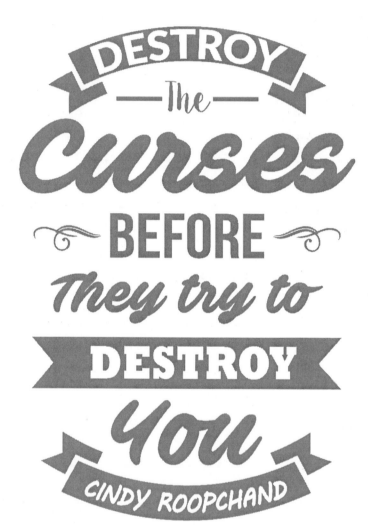

DESTROY
—The—
Curses
BEFORE
They try to
DESTROY
You
CINDY ROOPCHAND

17

BREAKING GENERATIONAL CURSES

The seventeenth key to becoming an overcomer is breaking generational curses. I remember someone asking me right after my miscarriage if I had ever heard of generational curses. It was the first time I had ever heard that term. The Bible says in Hosea 4:6, "My people are destroyed from lack of knowledge." Knowledge and awareness are crucial. The Bible tells us that people will suffer if they continue to walk in sin and ignorance of the Word of God.

"Now if a person sins and does any of the things which the Lord has commanded not to be done, though he was unaware, still he is guilty and shall bear his punishment" (Leviticus 5:17 NASB). "Hear you earth: I am bringing disaster on this people, the fruit of their schemes, because they have not listened to my words and have rejected my law" (Jeremiah 6:19). It is so important to know the Word of God because we will be judged by His Word.

Generational curses are sins or curses that are passed down from one generation to another. It could be sins or negative things you inherited from your forefathers. The Bible informs us that the sins of the parents can cause the same contamination to be passed down to their children. "I lavish unfailing love to a thousand generations. I forgive iniquity, rebellion, and sin. But I do not excuse the guilty. I lay the sins of the parents upon their children and grandchildren; the entire family is affected - even children in the third and fourth generations" (Exodus 34:7 NLT). "Our fathers have sinned and are not and we have borne (been punished for) their iniquities" (Lamentations 5:7 KJV, parenthesis added).

From these scriptures, God is warning us that He is a jealous God and He will punish the children for the sins of their fathers to the third and fourth generation of those who hate Him. It is important to be aware of generational curses, especially if you come from a family that did not serve the Lord.

The effects of sin can pass down from one generation to the next. If you come from a family that has a sinful lifestyle, you are mostly like going to repeat that same sinful lifestyle. An example of a generational curse is that my father was a worrier, so I became a worrier. So, basically, the strongholds or the generational demons your parents or family dealt with will afflict you, too. It is a bondage that is handed down to you through your bloodline. Unless you deal with these generational curses, the enemy will have the legal right to remain in your bloodline and attack the next generation.

In addition, unconfessed sins open the door to the enemy. The enemy is fully aware of the openings we have for him to have access to our lives. He knows the sins of our forefathers and ancestors. Therefore, it is crucial for you to be aware of these generational sins and expose these demons. Be a bloodline breaker and kick these demons out of your life and your future generation. I knew these generational curses needed to end with me!

You may ask, "What's the remedy for generational curses?" Repentance! In the Bible whenever the Israel or God's chosen people turned away from sin or worshiping idols to serving the One True Living God, the curse was broken, and God saved them (See Judges 3:9; 1 Samuel 12:10-11). Although

God did warn He would visit Israel's sins to the third and fourth generations, in the next verse He promised that He would show love to a thousand generations of those who love Him and keep His commandments (See Exodus 20:6). We serve a merciful God and His grace lasts a thousand times longer than His wrath.

Salvation through Jesus Christ is the primary way to break generational curses. The Bible says, Jesus Christ came and died on the cross conquering the enemy, so that we could be set free from any curse. "Christ has redeemed us from the curse of the law, having become a curse for us (for it is written, 'Cursed *is* everyone who hangs on a tree') (Galatians 3:13 NKJV). Therefore, the blood of Jesus is stronger than any of these generational curses.

When you accept Jesus as your Lord and Savior, you come into covenant with Him by being baptized and receiving the Holy Spirit. You have a new birth experience and you become a child of God. You are adopted into the Kingdom of God. Being a born-again believer gives you a new spiritual DNA and allows the blood of Jesus to cover you. Your bloodline is now connected to Jesus Christ, so you are no longer under the bloodline and curses of your forefathers.

I believe most of your generational curses are broken automatically when you become born again. However, you should confess or renounce the sins of your forefathers, so they can be broken once-for-all and you can be set free. I remember seeking the Lord about my family history. I asked Him to show me any demons that may be in my bloodline from my maternal and paternal side. I began to pray and ask God to reveal and expose any ancestral demons I may have inherited, and I began to repent and cast these demons out of my life. For God has given us authority over all the power of the enemy and we can walk among snakes and scorpions and crush them. Nothing will injure us (See Luke 10:19).

We cannot afford to be ignorant of the attacks of the enemy. We need to be aware of his tactics. The Bible says, "... lest Satan should take advantage of us; for we are not ignorant of his devices" (2 Corinthians 2:11 NKJV). Satan "plots against the just and gnashes at him with his teeth" (Psalm 37:12 NKJV).

Once you become a born-again believer and give your life to God, you are crossing over from darkness to light. The enemy now knows the power and the authority you hold. Therefore, he is plotting and planning on how to destroy you or prevent you from walking in your God-ordained purpose. He is looking for any way he may gain entrance into your life. Unconfessed sins and generational curses are ways he may gain access. This why it is crucial for you to expose these sins, repent and kick the enemy out of your life and bloodline!

KEY PROMISE SCRIPTURE

"Christ redeemed us from the curse of the law by becoming a curse for us, for it is written, cursed is everyone who is hung on a pole"
(Galatians 3:13)

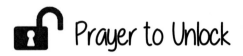 # Prayer to Unlock

I confess and repent of each and every sin, known or unknown, that I have committed, and I accept Jesus' forgiveness. He hung on the cross and redeemed me from the curse of the law. In the name of Jesus Christ, I confess all the sins of my forefathers, and by the Blood and the Authority of Jesus Christ, I now break the power of every curse passed down to me through my bloodline or ancestral line. Jesus, I ask You to send Your warring angels now to completely disarm and dismantle every curse from life. Through the blood of Jesus Christ, I am free!

I now claim every spiritual blessing that my Heavenly Father has given to me in Jesus Christ (Ephesians 1:3). I ask these things in the mighty name of Jesus Christ. Amen.

Declarations

I Decree and Declare I am no longer under any generational curses.

I Decree and Declare the Blood of Jesus has broken every curse in my life.

I Decree and Declare that I have shut the door to the enemy.

I Decree and Declare I am a bloodline breaker.

I Decree and Declare I have a new inheritance through Jesus Christ.

 Key Points

"Write the vision and make it plain on tablets, that he may run who reads it."
(Habakkuk 2:2 NKJV)

Jot down any key points or key ideas you gained from this section...

Think About It: How can I apply these keys in my life?

_____

_____

_____

_____

_____

_____

_____

_____

_____

_____

_____

_____

_____

_____

_____

_____

_____

_____

_____

_____

DECEPTION *is a*

DEMONIC

trap.
Don't

GET CAUGHT

IN IT!

CINDY ROOPCHAND

18

DECEPTION – THE ENEMY IS A LIAR

The eighteenth key to becoming an overcomer is to recognize deception and come out of it. Most of the time you do not know you are being deceived until someone reveals the truth to you. For many years I walked in deception. I believed the lies of the enemy. He has been deceiving mankind since the beginning of time. Eve is a perfect example of spiritual deception when the serpent asks her "Did God really say ...?" Then he tempts her with the attractiveness of the fruit and what she could gain from eating from the tree. She knew what God had said. Unfortunately, the enemy was able to deceive her and seduce her into disobeying God.

The serpent is cunning and clever. He is the master manipulator and tempter. The Bible calls him the "father of lies" (John 8:44). Satan knows how to make sin look good. Eve was lied to and she believed the lie. She believed that eating the forbidden fruit could have given her a better life.

The Bible says in 2 Corinthians 4:4, "The god of this age has blinded the minds of unbelievers, so they cannot see the light of the gospel of the glory of Christ." Rejecting God and His Word opens the door to spiritual deception. Some people are tempted by their "own evil desire" (James 1:14). Self-satisfaction and walking in your own desires make satan's deceptions more compelling. It is important to understand that spiritual deception comes from what we choose to believe.

"Even after Jesus had performed so many signs in their presence, they still would not believe in him" (John 12:37). The people decided not to believe in Jesus despite the sign, wonders and miracles He had performed. Their unbelief was willful despite the evidence. It is dangerous for believers to exchange the truth for a lie. When you give up the truth, you are mostly likely going to be deceived to believe anything.

The enemy tends to deceive us through temptations. However, you can overcome his temptations just like Jesus did when He was tempted in the wilderness. Let's take a look at how Jesus overcame the enemy:

> *Jesus, full of the Holy Spirit, left the Jordan and was led by the Spirit into the wilderness, where for forty days He was tempted by the devil. He ate nothing during those days, and at the end of them He was hungry. The devil said to him, "If you are the Son of God, tell this stone to become bread." Jesus answered," It is written: 'Man shall not live on bread alone but by every word of God.'"*

> *The devil led him up to a high place and showed him in an instant all the kingdoms of the world. And He said to him," I will give you all their authority and splendor; it has been given to me, and I can give it to anyone I want to. If you worship me, it will all be yours."*

> *Jesus answered," It is written: 'Worship the Lord your God and serve him only."*

> *The devil led him to Jerusalem and had him stand on the highest point of the temple. "If you are the Son of God,' he said, 'throw yourself down from here. For it is written:*

'He will command his angels concerning you to guard you carefully; they will lift you up in their hands, so that you will not strike your foot against a stone.'"

Jesus answered, "It is said: 'Do not put the Lord your God to the test.'" When the devil had finished all this tempting, he left him until an opportune time (Luke 4:1-13).

The enemy tends to deceive us by questioning us. He first tempted Jesus by asking Him if He was the Son of God to command the stones to become bread (See Luke 4:3). The enemy likes to question our identity in God. He wants us to forget we are a new creature in Christ and have a new identity in Christ. He is aware of the power and the authority we have as daughters and sons of the King of Kings and the Lord of Lords. He wants us to question the sonship we inherited from being a born-again believer.

How did Jesus respond to the enemy? By quoting the Word of God. The Word of God is the greatest weapon we have against the enemy. This is why it is crucial to know and apply the Word of God. If you know the Truth which is the Word, then you cannot be deceived.

Next, the enemy tried to tempt Jesus by offering Him the power and the riches and glory of this world if He would bow down and worship him. Jesus responded to him that it is written to worship and serve God only. The enemy wants us to bow down to him, serve him and worship him. He is a glory thief. Satan will offer you the riches of this world in exchange for your soul. Don't fall for it. The riches you will receive from your Heavenly Father cannot be compared to riches of this world. Don't ever compromise the truth, your salvation, and your God-ordained purpose for an opportunity from the enemy. When we know the Word of God and seek the will of God, we can discern the lies of the enemy.

Then the enemy came a third time to tempt Jesus, this time tempting Him to kill Himself. He brought Jesus to Jerusalem and had Him stand on the highest point of the temple. He asked Jesus, "If you are the Son of God, throw yourself down from here" (Luke 4:9). If the enemy cannot defeat you, he wants you dead. He knows the power you hold and the lives you will reach for the Kingdom of God. This is why he wants to deceive us and keep us in bondage.

Remember the enemy "comes only to steal, kill, and destroy" (John 10:10). He wants to steal your destiny, kill and destroy you. 1 Peter 5:8 declares, "Be alert and of sober mind. Your enemy the devil prowls around like a roaring lion looking for someone to devour." It is imperative that you are aware of the deception of the enemy. You must be on guard and filled with the Word of God so you cannot be deceived by the lies of the enemy.

KEY PROMISE SCRIPTURE

"Be not deceived, God is not mocked, for whatsoever a man soweth, that shall he also reap. For he that soweth to his flesh shall reap corruption; but he that soweth to the Spirit shall reap life everlasting"
(Galatians 6:7-8 KJV)

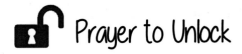 # Prayer to Unlock

Father, in Jesus' name, reveal to me any deception I may have in my life. I do not want to walk in spiritual blindness but in truth. Remove and reveal any satanic traps in my life. I want to be free from all the lies of the enemy, fear, lust of the flesh, lust of the eye, and the pride of life that may cause me to sow into my flesh and reap corruption. I repent of any association or agreement with the spirit of deception. I cast this spirit out by the precious Blood and mighty name of Jesus.

Declarations

I Decree and Declare I am no longer deceived by the enemy.

I Decree and Declare the scales have been removed from my eyes.

I Decree and Declare I no longer walk in spiritual blindness.

I Decree and Declare I walk in truth.

I Decree and Declare I walk in the discernment of the Lord.

 Key Points

"Write the vision and make it plain on tablets, that he may run who reads it. "
(Habakkuk 2:2 NKJV)

Jot down any key points or key ideas you gained from this section...

Think About It: How can I apply these keys in my life?

_____

_____

_____

_____

_____

_____

_____

_____

_____

_____

_____

_____

_____

_____

_____

_____

_____

_____

_____

_____

WISDOM

★ ★ ★ ★ ★

and

REVELATION

★ *Give us* ★

DIVINE

INSTRUCTIONS

CINDY ROOPCHAND

19

WISDOM AND REVELATION

The nineteenth key to becoming an overcomer is to walk in wisdom and revelation from the Lord. Wisdom allows you to overcome any attacks of the enemy. It guides and allows you to make wise decisions. Wisdom keeps you away from the plots and plans of the enemy. It shows you the path of life (See Psalm 16:7-11). Wisdom enables you to walk safely in your God-ordained purpose and not stumble. Proverbs 9:10-11 declares, "The fear of the Lord is the beginning of wisdom and the knowledge of the Holy One is understanding. For through wisdom your days will be many, and years will be added to your life." If you want wisdom, you need to fear the Lord, to honor, reverence, and be obedient to Him.

The spirt of wisdom allows you to operate with the mind of God. It gives you divine direction, instruction and strategies. In God you will find hidden treasures of wisdom and knowledge (See Colossians 2:3). The Bible says, wisdom is better than gold and understanding is better than silver (See Proverbs 16:16). It also says, "He gives wisdom to the wise and knowledge to those who have understanding" (Daniel 2:21 ESV).

Wisdom gives us insight and understanding. It allows us to walk in discernment so we can identify what is right or wrong and make Godly decisions. It is imperative for us to ask and pray for the wisdom of God daily. James 1:5 (NKJV) declares, "If any of you lacks wisdom, let him ask of God, who gives to all liberally and without reproach, and it will be given to him."

If you want Godly wisdom you also need to walk in obedience. Proverbs 2:7 (NKJV) states, "He stores up sound wisdom for the upright. He is a shield to those who walk uprightly." Proverbs 3:6 (NKJV) says, "In all your ways acknowledge Him, And He shall direct your paths." When we acknowledge God in everything we do, He will give us wisdom and direction.

Another way to gain wisdom from God is by our humility. "When pride comes, then comes shame, but with the humble is wisdom" (Proverbs 11:2 NKJV). When we humble ourselves before God, He uploads His ideas and thoughts into our minds.

The Book of Proverbs gives us wisdom and suggestions for powerful living. God asked King Solomon what he wanted, and he asked for wisdom (See 1 Kings 3:5-14). King Solomon's request pleased the Lord. Not only did He make King Solomon wise, but He also gave him great riches and power. Most of the Book of Proverbs is written by King Solomon.

The Bible says in Proverbs 4:5-6: "Get wisdom, get understanding; do not forget my words or turn away from them. Do not forsake wisdom, and she will protect you; love her and she will watch over you." When we read God's Word and apply it in our lives, we gain wisdom. Wisdom guides and protects us. It gives us Godly counsel to make the right choices or decisions. God is the Spirit of Truth and He is the One that will lead you into the path of righteousness. He is the One that created you and He is the One that will show you what your calling or purpose is. When you trust in God, in His Word, and in His instruction, you will walk wisely into your destiny.

If you want to gain Godly wisdom, you need to plant yourself in the Word of God.   Proverbs 2 explains the moral benefits of wisdom. Read it and see what insights you may gain from this proverb.

Proverbs 2: Moral Benefits of Wisdom

My son, if you accept my words
and store up my commands within you,
turning your ear to wisdom
and applying your heart to understanding—
indeed, if you call out for insight
and cry aloud for understanding,
and if you look for it as for silver
and search for it as for hidden treasure,
then you will understand the fear of the Lord
and find the knowledge of God.
For the Lord gives wisdom;
from his mouth come knowledge and understanding.
He holds success in store for the upright,
he is a shield to those whose walk is blameless,
for he guards the course of the just
and protects the way of his faithful ones.

Then you will understand what is right and just
and fair—every good path.
For wisdom will enter your heart,
and knowledge will be pleasant to your soul.
Discretion will protect you,
and understanding will guard you.

Wisdom will save you from the ways of wicked men,
from men whose words are perverse,
who have left the straight paths
to walk in dark ways,
who delight in doing wrong
and rejoice in the perverseness of evil,
whose paths are crooked
and who are devious in their ways.

Wisdom will save you also from the adulterous woman,
from the wayward woman with her seductive words,
who has left the partner of her youth
and ignored the covenant she made before God.
Surely her house leads down to death
and her paths to the spirits of the dead.
None who go to her return
or attain the paths of life.

Thus you will walk in the ways of the good
and keep to the paths of the righteous.
For the upright will live in the land,
and the blameless will remain in it;
but the wicked will be cut off from the land,
and the unfaithful will be torn from it.

God reveals Himself to us in various ways. Some gain revelation through dreams, visions, nature, God encounters, Jesus, and through the written Word of God. Most of us gain revelation or insight from His Word. The Word of God is inspired, profitable, and sufficient (See 2 Timothy 3:16-17). The Word of God is living and active (See Hebrews 4:12). The Bible reveals the mind of God, the plans of God and the heart of God. When you read the Word of God, ask Him for special insight, understanding or revelation.

> "God, reveal Your secrets unto us (Daniel 2:28). Lord let Your Word be revealed unto us. (1 Samuel 3:7). Allow us to receive visions and revelations of the Lord (2 Corinthians 12:1). Impart an abundance of revelation in our lives (2 Corinthians 12:7). God, allow me to understand the deep things of You (1 Corinthians 2:10). God enlighten my eyes with Your Word (Psalm 19:8)."

Wisdom and Revelation are powerful keys to every overcomer's needs. Seek the wisdom and the counsel of God. Stay on the Word of God. Ask for daily wisdom and revelation and watch how God directs your step.

KEY PROMISE SCRIPTURE

"That the God of our Lord Jesus Christ, the Father of glory, may give to you the spirit of wisdom and revelation in the knowledge of Him"
(Ephesians 1:17 NKJV)

🔓 Prayer to Unlock

Lord, You said in Your Word that You store up wisdom for the upright (See Proverbs 2:7). Help us to walk uprightly in the path of righteousness. Lord, help us to be obedient to the Word of God and apply Biblical principles to our lives. Father, give us wisdom, knowledge and understanding to make wise decisions. Your Word says, "The fear of the Lord is the beginning of wisdom, and the knowledge of the Holy One is understanding, For by Me your days will be multiplied, and years of life will be added to you" (Proverbs 9:10-11 NKJV). God, help us to honor You by putting You first in our lives so that we may live long and prosperous lives. God, we know that in You and in Your Word are hidden all the gems "the treasure of wisdom and knowledge" (Colossians 2:3). Help us to find these hidden treasures so we can be rich in Your wisdom and knowledge. We ask these things in Jesus' name.

Declarations

I Decree and Declare that I seek Godly wisdom and He will direct my path.

I Decree and Declare I will ask for Godly wisdom daily.

I Decree and Declare I will search for the Wisdom of God in the Word of God.

I Decree and Declare I will make wise decisions.

I Decree and Declare God will increase my wisdom and knowledge.

163

 Key Points

"Write the vision and make it plain on tablets, that he may run who reads it. "
(Habakkuk 2:2 NKJV)

Jot down any key points or key ideas you gained from this section...

Think About It: How can I apply these keys in my life?

_____

_____

_____

_____

_____

_____

_____

_____

_____

_____

_____

_____

_____

_____

_____

_____

_____

_____

_____

WHEN
GOD POURS
DOWN HIS
FAVOR UPON YOU
NOTHING CAN
★ STOP THE ★
BLESSINGS
HE HAS IN STORE FOR YOU

CINDY ROOPCHAND

20

FAVOR

The twentieth key is all about favor. When you are favored by the Lord, you can overcome any circumstance. Favor is defined as "an act of kindness beyond what is due or is the usual liking for someone or something." It also means "to gain approval, support, preference for or preferential treatment." When we believe in Jesus and come into covenant relationship with Him, we receive the gift of God's favor. God loves to favor His children. When we walk by faith and believe God for the impossible, He releases His favor upon us.

God searches for those who love Him and are obedient to His commands so that He can grant them favor, bless them, and lead and protect them (See Psalm 37:23; Proverbs 3:5-6). At the same time, nowhere in the Bible does it state that everyone who is healthy and prosperous has found favor in God's eyes. Neither does it say that those who are favored by God will never suffer hardship. The Bible mentions many people who had the Lord's favor, yet suffered and had to overcome difficulties. There are so many generals of faith that the Bible mentions as being favored but had to overcome obstacles, for example, Joseph and Mary (Luke 1:28), Daniel (Daniel 10:19), Moses (Exodus 32:11; 33:13) and Noah (Genesis 6:8).

These Bible heroes were able to be overcomers because they knew God was with them and nothing could happen to them apart from His good purpose (See Romans 8:28). For He said He will never leave you nor forsake you and no weapon formed against you shall prosper (See Hebrews 13:5; Isaiah 54:17). These Bible Overcomers knew they had God's eyes and ears with them as they walk through dark valleys (See Psalm 34:15) and recognized that their struggle to remain true to Him would not go unrewarded (See Matthew 10:42; Revelation 2:10).

God's favor can be felt in a believer's spirit. It gives us a sense of peace to know that God is in control and has our best interests at heart. For He says in the Book of Jeremiah 29:11, "For I know the plans I have for you, declares the Lord plans to prosper you, and not to harm you, to give you hope and a future." When we walk in God's favor, we can rest in the quiet confidence that our sins are forgiven (See Romans 4:7), we are in the plan of God (See Psalm 86:11) and that He is there for us at all times (See Isaiah 41:10; Matthew 28:20).

To sum up, it is important for us to seek God's favor, to humble ourselves before Him and be obedient to Him. We need to seek Him not only for the blessings He gives but because He is God. We need to totally submit our mind, body, heart, spirit and soul to Him. When we put God and His agenda first, this will open the door of favor to us.

KEY PROMISE SCRIPTURE

"For the Lord God is a sun and shield the Lord bestows favor and honor; no good thing does he withhold from those whose walk is blameless"
(Psalm 84:11)

🔓 Prayer to Unlock

Lord, I thank You for Your Divine Favor. I know with You by my side, I can live an abundant life. I know You will supply all my needs. I thank You for favor with You and with men and women. I thank You that the first thing people come in contact with is my favor shield. Lord, I trust that no good thing will be withheld from me as I walk humbly and uprightly before You. I thank You that Your favor goes ahead of me and prepares the way. I thank You for preferential treatment everywhere I go. I am confident Your favor is on me. I have great expectations for this day and for the rest of my life. I pray these things in Jesus' Name. Amen.

Declarations

I Decree and Declare God's favor surrounds me.

I Decree and Declare I am blessed and highly favored.

I Decree and Declare that I am walking in Divine Favor.

I Decree and Declare I have supernatural favor with God and with everyone I come in contact with.

I Decree and Declare God's favor is opening up doors of opportunity for me.

 Key Points

"Write the vision and make it plain on tablets, that he may run
who reads it."
(Habakkuk 2:2 NKJV)

Jot down any key points or key ideas you gained from
this section...

Think About It: How can I apply these keys in my life?

_____
_____
_____
_____
_____
_____
_____
_____
_____
_____
_____
_____
_____
_____
_____
_____
_____

YOUR TESTIMONY Can Unlock PEOPLE SO FREE THEM!

Cindy Roopchand

21

TESTIFY – GO TELL THE WORLD

The twenty-first key to being an overcomer is to go and share the gospel with others. Your story can change someone's life. Your testimony can unlock someone's prison doors. Share what God did in your life and how He changed it. We should be a witness to God's transforming power. When you love Jesus, you will share His love with others. When we think about what He has done for us and how He has forgiven our sins and given us a new life in Him, we should be consumed with such gratitude and love that it overflows to others. We should plant the seeds of the gospel in others' lives. When we share our stories, it reminds us of the goodness of the Lord. It allows us to look back and see how much God has done for us and continues to do.

We should be a witness for Jesus because He commanded and commissioned us to do so. "He said to them, 'Go into all the world and preach the gospel to all creation'" (Mark 16:15). The Bible also states, "Then Jesus came to them and said, 'All authority in heaven and on earth has been given to me. Therefore, go and make disciples of all nations, baptizing them in the name of the Father, and of the Son, and of the Holy Spirit and teaching them to obey everything I have commanded you. And surely, I am with you always, to the very end of the age.'" (Matthew 28:18-20).

I encourage you to share the message of love and hope with others. When we share our faith, we fulfill our commission to be ambassadors for the gospel of Christ (See 2 Corinthians 5:20). God loves each and every one of us. His heart breaks for the lost – and so should ours. We should have compassion for the hopeless and for the ones that do not know

Jesus. We need to give them hope by sharing our story, especially how He saved us when we were lost. We should tell others how Jesus made us whole when we were broken. How He accepted us when we were rejected. How He healed and delivered us. How He set us free.

The Bible states, "The Lord is ... not willing that any should perish, but that all should come to repentance" (2 Peter 3:9 KJV). God doesn't want any of us to perish without being in a right relationship with Him. God's desires should be our desires. He loves us and we should share the love of God with others. We have the responsibility to share the good news and bring light to someone's darkness. We are God's hands, and feet. We are to give and carry the gospel. We are His mouthpiece, so we need to open our mouths and share our stories. We need to be obedient and share Him with the world.

Souls and lives are depending on you to share your story. You could be the reason someone gets their breakthrough. People's eternal destinies might be depending on you. I heard an evangelist share a message that people's blood might be in your hands if you don't open your mouth and share what God has done in your life. People need to know that God is not a respecter of person. If He can save us, He can save them, too.

I don't want anyone's blood on my hands, and this is the reason I overcame my fears and opened my mouth and shared my story. Your story can save someone's life, so share it.

KEY PROMISE SCRIPTURE

"And they overcame him by the blood of the Lamb, and by the word of their testimony..."
(Revelation 12:11 KJV)

🔓 Prayer to Unlock

Jesus, I thank You for rescuing me when I was drowning in my sins and sorrows. Thank You for Your transformation power and for giving me a new life. My testimony is not my story, but it is now Your story. Help me to boldly and courageously share it with others. Remove any fears, doubts, and blockages that will try to hinder me from sharing my testimony of Your goodness. You said in Mark 5:19, "Go home to your own people and tell them how much the Lord has done for you, and how he has had mercy on you." You also tell us to share our testimony in 1 Peter 3:15, "Always be prepared to give an answer to everyone who asks you to give the reason for the hope that you have."

Father God help me to be obedient in sharing my testimony with others. I know when I tell my story, it will glorify You. Thank You for opportunities to share my testimony. I ask these things in Jesus' Name, Amen.

Declarations

I Decree and Declare I will share my story.

I Decree and Declare that I will boldly share the gospel.

I Decree and Declare that I will go and tell others about the goodness of God in my life.

I Decree and Declare I will encourage someone by sharing my testimony on how God made me an overcomer.

 Key Points

"Write the vision and make it plain on tablets, that he may run who reads it. "
(Habakkuk 2:2 NKJV)

Jot down any key points or key ideas you gained from this section...

Think About It: How can I apply these keys in my life?

_____

_____

_____

_____

_____

_____

_____

_____

OVERCOMERS **SEE** THE RESURRECTED

JESUS *fighting* **THEIR BATTLES**

Cindy Roopchand

22

OVERCOMERS USE THEIR KINGDOM EYES

The twenty-second key to becoming an overcomer is seeing Jesus with your kingdom eyes or having a revelation of who Jesus really is. The returning Jesus is revealed to us in the Book of Revelation through the Apostle John: *"Look, he is coming with the clouds, and every eye will see him, even those who pierced him, and all the peoples on will mourn because of him, so shall it be! Amen. 'I am the Alpha and the Omega,' says the Lord God, 'who is and who was, and who is to come, the Almighty'"* (Revelation 1:7-8).

> *I turned around to see the voice that was speaking to me. And when I turned, I saw seven golden lampstands, and among the lampstands was someone like a son of man, dressed in a robe reaching down to his feet and with a golden sash around his chest. The hair on his head on was white like wool, as white as snow, and his eyes were like blazing fire. His feet were like bronze glowing in a furnace, and his voice was like the sound of rushing waters. In his right hand he held seven stars, and coming out of his mouth was a sharp, double-edge sword. His face was like the sun shining in all its brilliance. When I saw him, I fell at his feet as though I was dead. Then he placed his hands on me and said 'Do not be afraid, I am the First and the Last. I am the Living One, I was dead and now look, I am alive for ever and ever! And I hold the keys of death and Hades'* (Revelation 1:12-18)

Overcomers, we need to see the Jesus that John saw. This is not the baby Jesus the world witnessed in the manger, the Lamb of God version we celebrate at Christmas. I am talking about Jesus the Lion of Judah, the One the Book of Revelation describes as the One that is returning in power and majesty. The Bible says, in the Book of Philippians 2:10-11, "that at the name of Jesus every knee should bow in heaven and on earth and under the earth, and every tongue acknowledge that Jesus Christ is Lord, to the glory of God the Father. "

Many of us are unaware of who Jesus is after His resurrection. You need to connect or be introduced to the Risen Christ. We honor and worship Him for whom His word declares Him to be. When you read the Book of Revelation, it gives you insight into who King Jesus is. This is the Jesus that is in control of the heavens and the earth. The One who is on the throne. It is the Jesus that will simply astound you when you have an encounter with Him. This is the overcoming Jesus who has won the war for us!

I believe God places victory within our reach – but not in our hands. You have to want it and claim it. When Jesus went on the cross and shed His blood, we gained the victory. He defeated every enemy and took all the power from the works of darkness. Colossians 2:15 says God disarmed them. They no longer have control over you; their weapons have been taken away; their authority has been taken away. But people are deceived by the enemy that he is in still control. People fear him instead of the one who can take your soul. Get your perspectives right – fear God, the One who can destroy the world in a blink of an eye!

The Bible says anyone who believes in Christ has overcome. 1 John 5:4-5 says, *"For everyone born of God overcomes the world. This is the victory that has overcome the world, even our faith. Who is it that overcomes the world? The one who believes that Jesus is the Son of God."* Christ has made every born-again believer an overcomer. However, it is up to us to claim it.

In the Book of Revelation, Jesus promised amazing rewards to those who overcome. Overcomers are promised that they will eat from the Tree of Life in Revelation 2:7. They will eat the hidden manna and be given a new name in Revelation 2:17. God is promising us that, when we overcome evil and stand on God's Word, we will have wisdom. He will provide for us. God gives us a new beginning, a fresh start. In Revelation 2:11, we are promised we will be unharmed by the second death. Overcomers have authority over the nations in Revelation 2:26. They will be made a permanent pillar in the house of God (See Revelation 3:12) and sit with Jesus on His throne (See Revelation 3:21).

So, don't stay in chains anymore when you know Jesus has bought your freedom with His precious blood. He who the Son sets free is free indeed! He has given us overcoming power. We must exercise the power given to us. Put it into practice and run with it.

When Jesus freely gave His life, we became overcomers! You need to change your perspective to the Jesus that is greater than the problems you may have. He is the Great I AM. He is the Jesus that has fire in His eyes and whose voice is like a roaring thunder: that is the Jesus you should relate to. Stop looking at how big your problem is and start looking at how big your God is. You need to adjust your vision to the Risen Jesus. The One who Overcame the World. The One Who Defeated All of Our Enemies. This is the Jesus that is returning for His People. This is the Jesus that gives us the victory and is the One who causes us to triumph. Once you gain a revelation of who the Resurrected Jesus is you, are positioning yourself to overcome.   He is the reason we can become overcomers today! Jesus is the ultimate key that unlocks the overcomer in you! Use your kingdom eyes and begin to declare you are an overcomer through Jesus Christ!

KEY PROMISE SCRIPTURE

"I have said these things to you, that in me you may have peace. In the world you will have tribulation. But take heart, I have overcome the world"
(John 16:33 ESV)

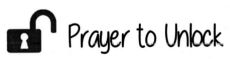 Prayer to Unlock

You are the Alpha and the Omega, the Beginning and the End. You are the Christ and the Creator. You are my Counselor and my Teacher. Thank You for giving me overcoming power. Thank You for making me victorious and allowing me to

defeat all of my enemies. You are Jehovah Jireh, the One who provides for all my needs. You are Jehovah Nissi, the One who fights my battles. You are the King of Kings and the Lord of Lords. You are invisible, but I see You with my kingdom eyes through faith. And, yes, You are Jesus, the Name above all Names. I thank You for making me an overcomer. I will keep my eyes fixed on you, Risen Savior, as You fight all of my battles and give me the victory. In Jesus' Name, Amen.

 Key Points

"Write the vision and make it plain on tablets, that he may run who reads it. "
(Habakkuk 2:2 NKJV)

Jot down any key points or key ideas you gained from this section...

Think About It: How can I apply these keys in my life?

_____

_____

_____

_____

_____

_____

_____

_____

_____

_____

_____

CONCLUSION

We live in a world where we will all have to overcome various obstacles or trials. But we have a choice: to allow these difficult circumstances to overcome us or to overcome these difficult circumstances. The word of God calls us overcomers. I believe God wants us to have overcoming experiences to glorify Him. God gave us the tools to be overcomers. Recognize that you are victorious, and defeat is not an option. I pray that the keys in this book have unlocked the overcomer in you. God Bless!

OVERCOMER'S PROCLAMATION

We must have an overcoming mindset. You must shift your thinking. Know that opposition may be an opportunity to overcome. Know that you are overcomers!

- I am an overcomer.

- I am victorious.

- I am more than a conqueror.

- I can do all things through Christ who strengthens me.

- I am chosen.

- I am God's masterpiece.

- I am the head and not the tail.

- I am a child of the Most High God.

- I am fearfully and wonderfully made.

- I am blessed and highly favored.

- I am gifted and I am given all things.

- I am living by faith.

- I am protected.

- I am the righteousness of God.

- I am transformed.

OVERCOMER'S PROCLAMATION (CONT.)

- I am a vessel of glory and honor.
- I am a witness.
- I am a shining star.
- I am free in Christ.
- I am accepted by Christ.
- I am forgiven.
- I am loved.
- I am redeemed.
- I am significant and secure.
- I have the mind of Christ.
- I am wise.

OVERCOMER'S SCRIPTURE DIRECTORY

Afraid
Psalm 34:4, Matthew 10:28, 2Timothy 1:7, Hebrew 13:5-6

Anxious
Psalm 46, Matthew 6:19-34, Philippians 4.6, 1 Peter 5:6-7

Bitter
1Cor. 13

Defeated
Romans 8:31-39

Depressed
Psalm 34

Determination
Job 31:1, Mark 8:34-38

Discouraged
Psalm 23, Psalm 55:22, Matthew 5:11-12, Psalm 42:6-11,
2Corthians 4:8-18, Phil.4:4-7

Doubt
Hebrews 3:12, Hebrews 11, Matthew 8:26, James 1:5-7

Facing A Crisis
Psalm 121, Matthew 6:25-34, Hebrews 4:16

Faith
Luke 1:37, Hebrews 11:6, James 2:14-26

OVERCOMER'S SCRIPTURE DIRECTORY (CONT.)

Forgiveness
Isaiah 1:18, 1Chronicles 2, Colossians 3:13

Hope
2 Corinthians 4:17-18, Isaiah 40:31

Loneliness
Psalm 23, Hebrews 13:5-6, Matthew 28:20, Psalms 68:6,

Needing God's Protection
Psalm 27:1-6, Psalm 91, Phil. 4:19

Needing Guidance
Proverbs3:5-6, Psalm 32:8

Needing Peace
Romans 5:1-5, John 14:1-4, John 16:33, Phil 4:6-7

Overcome
1John1:4-9, Psalm 6, Romans 8:31-39,

Overwhelmed
Ephesians 6:10-12, Psalm 91:1-2, Matthew 6:34

Worry
Romans 16, Esther 4, Matthew 8

NOTES

1. https://www.merriam-webster.com/dictionary/
   overcomer
2. Google Search
   https://www.google.com/search?q=what+does+the+wor
   d+overcome+mean&oq=what+does+the+word+overc&aqs
   =chrome.1.69i57j0l5.11060j0j8&sourceid=chrome&ie=
   UTF-8

3. http://www.yourdictionary.com/overcome
4. Never Thirsty
   https://www.neverthirsty.org/bible-qa/qa-
   archives/question/what-does-overcome-mean-in-the-
   greek-language

5. https://kingshighway.org/inspiration/articles/rewards
   -overcoming/definition-of-an-overcomer/
6. https://www.gotquestions.org/Bible-overcomer.html
7. https://m.facebook.com/notes/apostle-paul-a-
   williams/the-7-places-jesus-shed-his-blood-their-
   significance/10152713338390585/

ABOUT THE AUTHOR

Cindy Roopchand is a woman of God, wife, mother of two boys, teacher, motivational speaker, Youtuber, entrepreneur, published author and the Founder of Glory Girls for Jesus, which is a ministry dedicated to empowering and equipping others to be all that God created them to be. Cindy has a passion for helping others and she believes in sharing her journey to encourage others along the way. She co-wrote the book, *Love Behind The Blue Line: Stories of Love, Courage, Hope and Legacy* and the E-book, *Glambitious Guide To Being A Mompreneur. In addition,* she started her own business called All Things Glory, LLC and she has been an elementary school teacher for over 14 years.

Cindy received her Bachelor of Arts degree from the University of Albany and a Master's in Education degree from the College of New Rochelle. She has been featured in Freed Magazine, Sheen Magazine, LWL Magazine, Bronze Magazine, Women in Business International; and appeared on Awesome God Radio, BXNews12, Chosen Faces, Police Wives of America and more. She is dedicated to inspiring and impacting others. Cindy is determined to make her mark on the world.

Contact Cindy Roopchand at:
www.cindyroopchand.com
Croopchand2@gmail.com
Follow Cindy on Social Media
Facebook: Glory Girls for Jesus and GraceMercy
Instagram: @glorygirlsforjesus
YouTube Channel: Glory Girls for Jesus